How to Make More Money
at Interior Design

How to Make More Money at Interior Design

By Robert L. Alderman

Published by Whitney Communications Corporation
850 Third Avenue, New York, N.Y. 10022

Distributed by Van Nostrand Reinhold Company Inc.
135 West 50th Street, New York, N.Y. 10020

ISBN 0-442-20876-6

Printed in U.S.A.

Designed by Madlyn W. Dickens

Published by Whitney Communications Corporation
850 Third Avenue, New York, N.Y. 10022

Distributed by Van Nostrand Reinhold Company Inc.
135 West 50th Street, New York, N.Y. 10020

Acknowledgments

To Lester Dundes, Sherman Emery, and Virginia
Evans for their encouragement and foresight.

Table of Contents

How to Make More Money
at Interior Design

Preface

This book is a practical guide to the financial aspects of an interior design business for those designers operating by themselves or in small firms. This book offers essential information to any interior designer who intends to manage his business, keep old clients, and attract new ones.

I am an attorney engaged in the legal counseling and financial management of very successful interior designers. Since 1974, I have represented some of the most prestigious members of New York's design community. I am the author of the column, "Business and Design," which appears bi-monthly in *Interior Design* magazine, the most important monthly design publication for both residential and corporate interior designers. The column has a question-and-answer format offering a detailed financial and legal analysis of common problems confronting designers. This book is the result of the overwhelming response to that column.

Read it carefully, lay it aside, and then read it again. Refer to it from time to time when you identify problems in your own business that I have discussed here. If you analyze what I have written and transpose the knowledge to problems in your own business, this book will help you make more money than you might imagine. It could also *save* you a small fortune from common, costly mistakes that I will show you how to avoid. There is no other book for interior designers in this area nor is there likely to be. Approach it with the seriousness it warrants, and you will make more money.

INTRODUCTION:

Creativity and Confusion
Why Designers Don't Make Money

Most interior designers complain that they aren't making any money or "enough" money. I am not necessarily referring to beginners. I am talking about the ones whose work appears in the best publications, whose designs are licensed for products, whose names are well known and highly respected. When asked why they have money problems, they might say, "My clients never pay the way they are supposed to," or "They promised to pay a minimum fee and then changed their minds," or "The contractor took advantage of me, and I got ripped off." In other words, they blame others for their misfortune; they refuse to learn what actually went wrong; and they fall into the same traps over and over again.

When I try to talk over financial matters with some of my clients, I often hear, "Please, I haven't got the energy to talk about money now. I freeze when I face figures. And besides, I am not that smart anyway—I'm really just an artist who does not possess superior intellectual abilities". Creativity simply cannot manifest itself without a certain amount of basic intelligence.

What I really am hearing is, "I'm bored, I don't understand; let someone else do it for me; I really don't want to be bothered."

Unfortunately, he or she has to be bothered. Without money today, designers can be in real trouble, especially as they advance into their late thirties and onward. To attract clients, one has both to be a success and to look the part.

Some designers try to short circuit the problem by hiring financial experts and delegating all authority to them. Wrong again. Using professionals to help manage a career is a very smart move. But the designer must become involved, understand what is being done, and call the shots in the end. After all, whose career is it anyway?

Designers don't usually think along these lines. Many do not have an extensive formal design education and, even if they do, they probably learned nothing about business or money management. Design schools are notorious for inadequately preparing their students to cope with the business world. I have met a number of recent interior design school graduates who have never even seen a purchase order for furniture.

Designers *must* begin to learn about all financial aspects of their business as early in their careers as possible. Knowledge creates awareness; awareness develops skills and expertise. And this education must start early for an important psychological reason as well.

When a designer realizes that he is unable to cope with money, he first feels only apathy and disinterest. However, as his career progresses and his financial problems become more complex, he then becomes afraid to involve himself in this aspect of his career *because* he believes that he is a failure at it.

Knowledge dispels fear. And if designers possess basic financial skills when their careers begin, their business abilities and acumen will become increasingly sophisticated as their creative talents continue to develop.

But how can one gain this knowledge? Because business courses in design schools are either unavailable or inadequate, I prefer to see students take some conventional business courses in universities or colleges that specialize in business administration. These teachers will provide a basic concept of what business is about, and the student is then free to generalize and apply his knowledge to a specific area.

Business is a science just as design is an art. Accounting is a vital area of this science. The principles of accounting show where the money goes. An understanding of one's expenditure patterns leads to financial responsibility. Other helpful courses would be those in basic business management. It is useful to understand the general principles of how businesses are run and to understand the techniques used.

Another method of learning about the design business is to work for companies where one can see first hand how to handle money and make financial decisions. Good jobs are often hard to come by, however, and salaries for newcomers are, typically, shockingly low. And, often when an employer finds that a young designer can handle a specific aspect of a job particularly well, he will restrict him to that one slot because of his productivity. It is then up to the designer to make sure that he sees as many phases of the business as possible to insure a complete overview of its financial operation.

And what about those designers who are already established? Experienced designers will simply have to reshape their attitudes and become involved with the professionals they hire to handle financial and legal matters. Once they establish a new pattern and incorporate "business" into their concept of "what they do," the light at the end of the tunnel will allow them to see the rewards which are there.

If a designer is uncertain as to whether he should re-evaluate his role as a businessman, I always ask him where he belongs on the continuum of the Creativity Scale of Achievement. At the bottom are the *members*. These are the designers who have not achieved artistic recognition or monetary success—they just get by. At the middle of the scale, there are the *players*. They are active, purposeful achievers. At the top of the scale, there are the *factors*. They influence others. Their accomplishments transcend their generation and leave indelible marks for the future. We all know who they are. They are at the apex. While many strive for such achievement, few of us ever get there. Recognition as a designer implies a certain amount of financial success. Designers need visibility. For example, a designer should work and live in a showcase that projects his design image. Designers have to entertain clients comfortably to gain their confidence and communicate their design philosophies. Therefore, money becomes significant as a means of perpetuating design ideas and careers.

Whether a designer becomes a factor can only be known after enough time passes. If he is satisfied with his category on the scale, then the manner in which he is pursuing his career is the right one. If he is dissatisfied with his rating, he must examine the areas that need the greatest improvement and tackle the problems with new inspiration. The designer must consider why he doesn't make enough money.

Obviously, you don't think that *you* make enough money or you wouldn't have read this far. Although nothing can substitute for a good financial education or for years of experience of managing the finances of an employer or your own, I have provided a detailed guide to help you become smarter and more financially informed in most residential and some corporate markets.

I will help you handle such areas as:

- Preparing a Letter of Agreement
- Charging a Client
- Running a Design Project with Other Professionals
- Dealing with Responsibility
- Reacting when a Client changes his Mind
- Avoiding a Legal Crisis
- Handling Trouble on the Job

All of these topics will be discussed with specific examples. Some of them will be explored by using a summary of a "past history." Examples of common problems will be introduced and followed up by complete explanations, which will include other related points. If a question demands a legal response, it will be fully answered. All alternatives will be explored. Legal remedies will be tempered by business policy.

Not all of this can be digested and absorbed after only one or two readings. The best tactic for quick application is to study those areas I have zeroed in on. Once the same or similar issue occurs in your own business, refer immediately to that section in the book. Repeating the process over a period of time will result in learning and developing new insights.

The information in the following chapters is extremely important. Of course, if you are at all experienced, you will be aware of an infinite number of possible variables that can change the course of how a situation should be handled. Obviously, all these variables cannot be discussed here. What you will learn are general principles and the rationale for their development. The axiomatic rules did not evolve in a vacuum. They evolved from application, adaptation, and re-use. All this, too, can be defined as insight.

An interior designer must develop the ability to handle money and operate a business in order to be successful. Most books on financial management for designers do very little to help develop a clear understanding. They summarize problems briefly but don't explain what methods can be used to solve them. Here, I have done the reverse. I have restricted the number of problem areas but have explained and analyzed those few thoroughly. Since many overlap, you will see how they repeat themselves in different subject areas.

In summary, a key to being successful is an ability to make money. To make money, education, knowledge, and experience are required. Insight is developed through the use of analysis.

This book analyzes some of your most pressing business problems. Use it properly and the operation of your own business will cease to be a dilemma. It will become instead a series of manageable problem areas. You will have more time, make more money and be more successful.

CHAPTER ONE:

Preparing a Letter of Agreement

One of the first things a client is likely to ask is, "How much do you charge?" and then "May I see a copy of your contract?"

Young designers are stunned by the frequency of these questions at such a premature level of the designer-client relationship. "After all," they say, "they want to know how much I charge and what my contract is like before they even take a look at my portfolio."

But look at these questions in a different light. I once asked a client of mine, a well-known architect, why certain run-of-the-mill architectural firms are selected over established architects who are known to be geniuses. "Because," he told me, "corporations are mainly concerned with having their buildings finished at budget and on time. They have to answer to stockholders and boards of directors. As long as the building fits the purposes for which it is intended, the overall quality of the design does not have the highest priority. These firms deliver as promised. Their clients know this and trust them."

Most interior design clients, especially those who are retaining the services of a professional for the first time, are usually unsophisticated about the field of design. Of course, they have varying tastes and preferences. They might know, for example, that they prefer some colors and textures to others or that they want a modern look, not a traditional one. But very often, the decisive factor for these clients is whether you look "professional." I assume that you are capable of discussing your philosophy of design with a prospective client, but a professional should also be able to present his financial posture in a positive way. Charging a client will be discussed in depth in the next chapter, but now, let's discuss preparing a letter of agreement.

I will show you how to make this letter look professional, how to present a business format while still preserving your design image, and how to protect yourself from financial loss as a result of unforeseen circumstances.

Sample concepts will be provided as segments of your letter of agreement. Professionals use different techniques to suit their particular needs. Some will be suitable for your use; others will not. A presentation of possible approaches will offer hints on the psychology involved in preparing a letter of agreement. This information will protect you and make you *look* professional even if you have never operated on a freelance basis before. If you are already conducting a business, you will receive confirmation on certain areas and will question others. You might realize that you have been operating without sufficient protection and see what you can do to limit potential liability from certain risks. If you are in the early stages of setting up your business, it may not be possible to be too stringent about some demands. However, as a more secure financial base is developed, you will then be able to gradually add more protection. Leverage with clients is important, and the letter of agreement is one of your most important levers. It defines responsibilities, obligations, and can often make or break you.

When Do You Present a Client With a Letter of Agreement?

Before discussing how to prepare it, it only makes sense to talk about when to produce it.

There are two schools of thought on this subject. You can have a "standard letter" ready to show a client with blank spaces to fill in his name and other details, or you can prepare each letter on an individual basis and not show it to the client until it is worked out and completed.

You have a strong advantage with a "standard letter." If the client is faced with a "fill-in-the-blanks-contract," he may feel, "Well, this is what he uses for everyone. It must be all right. I suppose if I want to hire him, I have to agree to the same terms that all the rest of his clients do. I may as well sign it."

There are two problems with this technique. Although you may develop a standard letter, it is most unlikely that you will have standard clients. Each will be different. If you show a client a "standard letter" but then decide to make changes for the project at hand, you might run into some heavy objections. Your client may feel that your changes are discriminatory and unreasonable deviations from your standard policy.

There is a second disadvantage. Timing is very important. Even though your letter of agreement will contain many standard clauses, many others will depend upon the project. It takes time, thought, and perhaps the help of another professional to prepare a letter of agreement, especially for a project of any size. This can cost money. Before going through all of this, you should be fairly sure that the client will actually be doing business with your office.

Generally, a prospective client will meet with you at least twice before deciding to hire you. Get as much "job input" as possible before supplying information about fees or letters of agreement. In some instances, this won't be a problem. You'll know exactly what you have to do, how much it will cost, and how you'll need to operate. You'll be able to talk business right away. But at other times, you won't be so sure.

When you are faced with a financial question you can't answer, stall. Remember, your client will always be more familiar with the particulars of his project than you will. He may come in, for example, with a set of floor plans or drawings, and say, "Okay, I want 'this', 'this,' and 'this.' How much do you charge, how much will the project cost, when will it be finished, and do you have a letter of agreement?"

This is a typical rapid-fire "businessman's approach." Everything you say will be remembered. When you are caught in these circumstances, say, "I really have to give this some thought. I have a business manager (or lawyer or accountant) that I have to talk about this with before I can give you an answer to that."

After the client has left your office, you can decide what you want to quote. Review things carefully and perhaps talk it over with another professional.

At the next meeting, advise your client about financial and other general business terms orally. If he accepts the terms and agrees to hire you, *then* prepare your letter of agreement.

Designers have frequently called me with this complaint. "I showed your letter of agreement to my new client," they say. "Before we prepared it, I told them about all the terms and they agreed. Now, they're objecting to everything all over again, and they don't want to sign it."

Nothing is foolproof. Some clients are tough. They'll say "yes" one minute and "no" the next. Generally, you should sound out a client thoroughly before submitting a letter of agreement unless you are absolutely positive about how you will operate in the given situation. Present the letter only when you're prepared and ready.

Why Use a Letter as a Format?

The use of a letter of agreement as opposed to a contract can be a key to your relationship with your client, especially in residential situations. A designer-client relationship is often very personal. Many clients expect not only an attractive series of rooms but a new life style. They may have harbored long-established fantasies about the way they want to live and work. The designer is the "genie" who is to fulfill their wishes. Accordingly, the first written encounter must provide all the elements necessary to define the new relationship; it should be presented in a very personal way. Therefore, a formal legal format is inappropriate. The language should not be stiff or legalistic; it should sound like you. Don't use "party of the first part," "whereas" or "forthwith." Dispose of that terminology, just say the same thing in layman's language.

A letter format does not affect the legality of your agreement. A letter of agreement is a contract with a different presentation. A more personal approach, however, does not have to sacrifice thoroughness, clarity, and a comprehensive treatment of the necessary areas. Say what you have to but in the right way.

Specify the Area To Be Designed

In the introductory paragraph, state the name of the client and the address of the space. In residential projects, list the number of rooms to be designed and describe them by name:

Dear Mr. and Mrs. Smith:
We are pleased to submit our letter of agreement describing our design and planning services for your apartment. The areas of your residence, 9000 Park Avenue, New York, New York, Apartment 23D, which relate to this agreement are the following:
   A. Entrance Foyer
   B. Library
   C. Living room
   D. Dining room
   E. Master Bedroom and Bath

This situation is a perfect example as to why it is important to be so specific. Obviously, the apartment is larger than the number of rooms listed. There would also be a kitchen, pantry, other bedrooms and bathrooms, etc. However, the Smiths are only interested in working on these rooms with their designer. If they wanted the entire apartment designed, you could omit specifically designating the rooms as shown in the second example:

> We are pleased to submit our letter of agreement describing our design and planning services for your entire residence at 9000 Park Avenue, New York, New York, Apartment 23D.

These distinctions can save you money, depending upon how you charge. If you charge a flat fee or a design fee plus a percentage of goods and construction, the amount of compensation is totally fixed in the first case and somewhat fixed in the second. Obviously, if the Smiths don't want the entire apartment designed at the start, you don't want other rooms, such as a kitchen, being added on later for no additional fee.

My clients who charge on a strictly "retail" or a "percentage" basis often argue, "As my fee has nothing to do with the number of rooms, I don't have to be specific. If they buy, I make money. If they don't, I make less."

That may be true. But there's yet another reason to be specific on a "room count." Frequently, clients try to pin down designers about completion dates. Presume that you told the Smiths that you could complete the five rooms in six months. If you had not been specific about the number of rooms and half way through the project they decided to add the kitchen to the project, at the end of six months you might not be finished. But the Smiths might object because you initially promised a six-month period and may even decide to withhold part of your fee until the work is finished. This sounds terribly unreasonable, but "fee withholding" is not uncommon. List rooms specifically unless you are designing the entire space. If an additional room is added later, the client will understand why the project will not be completed within the initial projected period.

This kind of precision is vital for commercial ventures. Identify the space that is being designed in every reasonably possible way. The following example is a typical description for a commercial office:

XYZ Corporation
5000 Madison Avenue
New York, New York

Attention: Clinton Jones, President

Dear Mr. Jones:
We are pleased to submit our letter of agreement describing our design and planning services for your offices consisting of the entire 21st floor at 9000 Madison Avenue, New York, New York. You have advised us that your space is approximately 10,000 usable square feet, which you will be permitted to subdivide. You have requested subdivision as follows:

1. Large reception area
2. Executive board room
3. Chief executive's office with private bath and kitchenette
4. Two additional executive offices without bath

5. Two small staff offices

6. Six secretarial areas

The same reasons for identifying spaces for design in residential projects apply here as well. However, listing can be even more important in commercial cases. Very often, designers will charge a basic commercial rate by the square foot. Obviously, then, the approximate footage should appear in the letter of agreement. In addition, designers charge higher percentages for more heavily decorated areas such as board rooms and executive offices. Accordingly, 15 per cent on purchases of goods and construction may be assessed on staff offices, and 20 per cent may be the rate for executive areas.

In summary, design areas should usually be identified and described at the beginning of your letter of agreement. It is generally wise to lay this foundation in order to make subsequent provisions understandable and enforceable.

Outline Project Development

After the introduction, explain in a concise, orderly manner the sequential development of design phases and your general method of operation. In other words, tell your client how you are going to run his project. This is one of the most important things he'll want to know. If he's worked with a designer before, he'll want to compare your technique with the previous designer's. If he's unfamiliar with the way a designer works, this will assure him that you use a thorough system.

Project development can be outlined in a list or described in one or two brief paragraphs. Avoid the list except for large, commercial projects where more formality is expected. The following example is typical of my clients:

As we have discussed, the project will be designed and supervised by (the designer) and other members of our staff. All plans, furnishings, and budget will be approved by you in advance.

Our general method of operation shall be as follows. Initially, we will consult with you to determine the requirements of each area of your residence to be designed. All areas will be surveyed and measured. Next, design plans and materials will be presented with a preliminary budget. Based upon your final approval and signature of the designs and renderings, the following interior architectural drawings will be prepared:

A. Cabinet work

B. Reflected ceilings

C. Painting and wall covering schedule.

All basic plans, drawings, schedules, and sketches will be reviewed with you and subject to your written approval. These items will then be submitted for competitive bidding to a contractor of your choice or ours. The quality and supervision of the work are the obligation of the contractor although we will provide any reasonable assistance and will visit the project, as necessary, to determine if the contractor is conforming to our drawings.

At this point, some observations are in order to help you prepare your own letter.

"Other members of your staff" may be working on the

project. Even if you don't have a partner, you may decide to hire an assistant—you never know. Clients often object if you don't handle every detail personally. If you warn them in advance that you may have to delegate some of the tasks to your assistant, it will help to prevent future problems.

If no detailed floor plan exists, you will have to measure the space or hire someone to do it for you. Let your client know this. Scaled drawings look very professional. Free-hand sketches are for amateurs.

You will interview your client to discuss requirements of the space. Some designers ask clients to submit a list of "musts" or "likes and dislikes." This doesn't have to be mentioned in the agreement itself, although it could be. Usually, the designer will explain this when he reviews the contract with the prospective client.

Once a tentative design is prepared—i.e., a floor plan is prepared containing a furniture layout, a color scheme is selected with sample fabrics, pictures of furniture, sketches of built-ins, etc.—the designer will make his visual presentation to the client.

In the example the visual presentation is simply called "design plans and materials." Some think it is more impressive to specify how elaborate their visual presentation will be. Others don't want to pin themselves down to exhaustive presentations, so they leave the wording very loose (as in the example) and then decide later how detailed they want to be.

As the example illustrates, some designers prepare a preliminary budget at the time of the visual presentation. If that's how you operate, mention it. To avoid wasting time, some designers will not prepare a budget until final selections are made. A "guess-estimate" is not considered a preliminary budget. If you want to mention general figures at the presentation, qualify your answers as uncertain. Put in writing only numbers that have been costed out with a fair amount of precision.

Once all preliminary stages are complete, prepare final architectural drawings or plans. The example lists three typical final sets of plans or drawings prepared by interior designers, i.e., cabinet work, reflected ceiling plan, painting and wallcovering schedule.

After the design has been completed, the drawings may have to be submitted to contractors for estimates. Many designers have their favorite general contractors and specialty craftsmen; however, in the letter of agreement, it is always smart to indicate that the plans will be sent out for competitive bidding. Often clients urge designers to work with whomever they like. However, let your client know that you have an open mind.

The final sentence in the example is most important. The quality of the work is the responsibility of the contractor, not the designer. You must visit the site to insure that your drawings are being complied with, but you are not responsible for faulty construction or inadequate workmanship. Of course, you will ultimately be the middleman to correct any reasonable problem, but don't let either the client or contractor try to pass the buck to you in the case of a costly mistake by the contractor.

These suggestions on outlining project development are based upon the general methods of operation of many designers I have counseled. However, every designer operates differently, and, very often, the same designer may substantially vary his procedure from one project to the next according to their different needs and requirements.

Although the example gives you an idea of what a project outline might contain, there cannot be a standard form. Here is how I handle it with my own clients.

When new clients ask me to prepare a letter of agreement, their general preconception is that I will put together a model package of standard clauses tailored for their needs. I advise that I don't do models and they should contact me when they have a new client ready to enter into an agreement. At that time, the designer and I, working with specific facts about the tangible project, prepare a letter of agreement.

When we arrive at the outline of project development section, I ask, "Now, what are you going to do on this project from start to finish?" Make a list. Take a new project and numerically list what you are going to do for that specific situation. Use my example in this chapter as a checkpoint. Then write it up in one or two cohesive paragraphs, generally less than 500 words. Every time you are about to prepare a new letter of agreement, check this list to see if you will be operating in a different way. Change the list as necessary to conform with the requirements of the specific project. This process gets easier over time.

Why place so much emphasis on a section that does not either protect against something or create income? The answer is easy. Outlining methods of operation helps create a professional image, the absence of which can lose you clients.

When clients approach designers, they are not only considering the extent of the design fee but also the quality of advice with regard to substantial expenditures on goods and services. They want, of course, to be certain that their money will be well spent and that the expenditures will be weighed carefully. When you present a letter of agreement to clients requesting an advance retainer or design fee, the right impression must be conveyed from the outset. When clients see the method of operation outlined in the agreement, they can visualize exactly how their project will be handled. They see that a businesslike as well as creative approach will be used to plan their project. Many very talented designers never become successful because they are unable to convince clients that they are responsible enough to handle the financial aspects of the job. A professional approach is essential to obtain the client's trust. Once you have that trust, you are more likely to be hired.

Insist on Written Client Approval

Always provide that clients must approve all their decisions in writing. In the previous section, Outlining Project Development, I used a design outline as an example. Notice that I discussed written approval at two stages of the project.

Because projects usually progress in phases, don't go from one to the next without the client's written approval. If the client approves your visual presentation e.g., when samples of merchandise and drawings are mounted on board-have him initial it. When a final budget is prepared and approved, have him sign it. This is especially important if the budget exceeds the original figure (which is typically the case) in order to prevent conflict. When purchase orders or estimates are obtained, have the client sign these also, even if he submits the deposit.

Be specific. Here is a good example:

You will be required to provide your written approval upon acceptance of the visual presentation, final budget, purchase orders, and all construction drawings.

Although this clause is one of the easiest to insert, it can end up being one of the most important. The significance of timely client approval will be apparent later when dealing with responsibility is discussed.

Purchases

There are three different purchasing methods:

1. Designer is the direct purchaser;
2. Designer purchases as an agent for the client;
3. Client makes purchases directly.

Any one of the three methods may be appropriate at different times.

For example, if you are basically decorating with little construction, you might want to charge retail, keeping your client unaware of your mark-up. When charging retail, designers generally purchase directly. In your agreement, state, "All purchases will be made at retail cost, and all purchasing transactions will be handled by my office." I will consider techniques for requesting payments when discussing other methods of purchasing.

If you charge on a "cost plus" basis, i.e., a percentage of

the cost of goods and construction, you may decide to act as a purchasing agent. Designers like that method as they can control the project by purchasing directly and limit their liability for ultimate payment by retaining their status as an agent. Suggested language when using this method is as follows:

All purchases will be made available to you at our wholesale cost, and our office shall act as your purchasing agent in this connection. We shall prepare all necessary purchase orders (deposit requests) and submit them to you for your written approval. Upon approval of purchase orders, payment shall be made as follows:

A. Full payment for wallpaper, fabrics, lighting fixtures, accessories, plants, and any retail items (i.e., flatware, china, crystal, linen and other household items) and design fees thereon;

B. Fifty (50%) Per Cent of wholesale cost and design fees for other furnishings and fixtures with the remaining balances due prior to delivery and installation;

C. Fifty (50%) Per Cent of wholesale cost and design fees on all labor and construction with the remaining balances due prior to completion.

Payments shall include sales tax, freight, and shipping charges on purchase orders and invoices for merchandise ordered for you.

Some design firms want the client to make the purchases directly. As designers, they need only prepare the specifications, and all the bookkeeping and liability are eliminated from their offices. Here is an example of how to provide for direct payment:

> All purchases will be made available to you at our wholesale cost. As you are the purchaser, all bills will be sent to you directly for payment. Although we will prepare the purchase orders, as the "purchaser", you will deal directly with the vendor on a proforma basis. We will not be held liable for any payment, including sales tax, freight, and shipping charges on purchase orders and invoices for any merchandise ordered for you.

Some designers further minimize their involvement in the purchasing process, especially when purchasing on a cost-plus basis. They add the following statement:

> Our role is to expedite and doublecheck your purchases and to follow up in case of loss or damage. Please bear in mind that we do everything to keep the furniture deliveries on schedule, but we cannot answer for those vendors who do not make the promised delivery dates. Just before "move-in," we compose a "punch list" of outstanding items and concentrate on expediting the delivery and installation of the same.

This may seem unimportant at first glance, but remember how some clients have reacted when furniture deliveries were a month late or more or when workmen suddenly failed to appear to complete jobs in progress. Most clients understand that such problems are bound to crop up on a job, but others become enraged and blame their designers for things that are totally beyond their control.

The previous example is a "disclaiming statement," a statement placed in a letter of agreement to minimize as much as possible the designer's responsibilities for purchases. Some designers refuse to disclaim, feeling that it is part of their responsibility to their clients to remain somewhat liable themselves.

I disagree. A designer may place himself in a risk-free position from a legal standpoint without abdicating any of his professional responsibilities. Disclaimer statements keep the designer off the hook in case the client decides not to pay balances on approved and ordered merchandise. This will be discussed in detail under *Dealing with Responsibility*.

Outside Purchases

After purchases have been discussed, I usually recommend the insertion of the following sentences:

> It is understood and agreed that all furnishings and construction will be purchased to implement the floor plan and architectural drawings submitted by our office. In the connection, we will agree to assist you in the purchase of the foregoing at our cost. However, in the event any such purchases are made or contracted for during the tenure of this agreement without our services or consultation, said purchases will be included in the total cost used as a basis on which all commissions are assessed.

The reason for this insertion is fairly obvious but can be best illustrated by the following hypothetical situation.

Suppose you and your client decide to purchase an antique armoire for the bedroom. For two months, you both scour antique dealers, furniture stores, and auction galleries but find nothing that seems to fit the client's taste or budget. Then, a month later, when visiting his residence for an installation, you see an armoire in the bedroom that looks amazingly similar to a number of pieces you had seen when shopping together. The client explains that it was a gift, an impulsive purchase, or manufactures any number of other stories. According to the clause we are discussing, the commission is payable to you regardless of how the armoire finally was acquired. To prevent any misunderstanding about what the client already owned before your work began, after your letter of agreement is signed, request a list of any furniture that may have a potential use on the project.

If you are charging a flat fee, obviously you won't need a clause of this nature. The client's purchases have nothing to do with your compensation, so how they are made has little to do with your financial arrangements. However, when your compensation is tied in to the goods and services bought, monitor the source of purchases. If your client refuses to agree to this sort of clause, be wary. He obviously intends to get as much free mileage out of your ideas as possible.

When I suggest this clause to new clients, they invariably ask two questions. The first is, "This clause only covers purchases made while I am working on the project.

After I finish, they can use my ideas and buy anything they want without paying my commission. Is there anything I can do about that?"

The answer to that, of course, is no. No contract, no matter how foolproof, can completely protect you from a dishonest client. However, most clients are not dishonest.

If you are doing a large project, generally your client will want as much of your input and supervision as possible. He'll want you to place the furniture as well as select it. The more dependent the client is upon your design judgment, the less likely he'll want an incomplete project before you leave.

The second question is, "Have you ever caught a client of a designer making an outside purchase and inserted the purchase into the decorator's budget so that he got his commission?"

The answer to that question is also no. But I'll tell you what *has* happened. Many designers constantly complained about losing commissions on outside purchases. Placing this clause in their letters of agreement for new clients stopped these problems. The clause is more for prevention than to cure. When prospective clients read this clause, they are put on guard immediately. They know that their designer will be watching all the purchases as they are made, which is generally enough to discourage any unsupervised purchasing.

Includable Items
Designers often work with architects, commercially and residentially, thereby resulting in a series of problems, discussed later when the role of the interior designer is more

fully explored.* Once you have read that section, reread this one for a deeper understanding.

When working with other professionals, particularly if your fee is based upon cost plus, clarify which items are included in your budget for commission purposes. Because architects and builders supply various standard features, list any items subject to your design fees that could possibly enter a gray area, as this example illustrates:

> With respect to includable items for our budget, it is agreed and understood that all items for the interior that are specified by our firm are included in the budget for commission purposes. This includes, but is not limited, to the following:
>
> 1. Custom plumbing and hardware fixtures;
> 2. Lighting and switching;
> 3. Wall coverings and interior painting schedule;
> 4. Window treatments;
> 5. Flooring and floor coverings;
> 6. All cabinet work, including kitchen cabinets, custom vanities, buffets, bookshelves, banquettes and upholstery, and custom interior doors

Once this list is in your agreement, be prepared for a hassle. The architect and general contractor are going to want these items in *their* budget, not yours. An interior designer is often involved with others who have, to some degree, overlapping roles, so setting up budget boundaries may

*See: Running a Project with Other Professionals

involve a power struggle. You must clarify your position before you start. Once you begin work, it is too late to bargain for everything to which you're entitled.

Fees

Regardless of how you charge your clients, provide a direct and complete explanation of what your fees will be in the letter of agreement. If you are vague or evasive, the client might hesitate to sign because the approach appears unbusinesslike or misleading.

I advise my clients never to *begin* their letter with a discussion of fees. Although no rigid rules of sequence exist, I would suggest the following:

1. Introduction
2. Specify design areas
3. Outline project development
4. Purchases
5. Outside purchasing clause
6. Purchases included in budget (when necessary)

First tell the client what you are going to do for him. Then, let him know how much it will cost. If you intend to charge retail, state as follows:

In consideration for my services, you will be charged retail or list price, quoted by vendors and craftsmen, for goods and services that I will purchase on your behalf.

When you present the agreement to your client, explain exactly what this means orally. Explain that "retail" or "list" is the price of goods and services charged by vendors and craftsmen. As a designer, you are entitled to a professional discount or wholesale price. The discount, the difference between the wholesale and retail price, will be your fee for services.

Here is an example of how many successful designers, who charge on a cost-plus basis, i.e., a percentage of the goods and construction, set forth their fees:

> My fee for work under this agreement is projected at $45,000, i.e., thirty (30%) percent of a projected budget of $150,000. $5,000 is payable upon signing of this agreement and is not refundable. The balance is payable in accordance with our schedule of payments attached to the agreement. In the event, during the tenure of this agreement, you determine to discontinue the use of our services on this project, all commissions will be due and payable with respect to any purchase orders of goods and construction that have been approved by you pursuant to your written acknowledgement on such purchase orders that have been issued by our office.
>
> It is understood that if the total cost of your project increases because of additions approved in writing by you, our fee shall increase proportionately, i.e., 30% additional design fee on all approved purchases to implement the additions to the project beyond $150,000. This written approval shall be indicated by your signature on all purchase orders exceeding the projected budget.

This is a very sophisticated way of discussing your fee when charging cost plus. It outlines the minimum cost of your services and approximates the estimate of the project based upon the client's needs and your design concept. Designers are often reluctant to be this specific so early in the relationship for fear of scaring the client away. They prefer to whet his appetite and lead him into spending money as the job continues. However, a minimum figure will dispel any notions that a design miracle can be worked for substantially less. Telling the basic truth at this time can head off possible future misunderstandings once design plans are complete and the budget is prepared.

If you feel strongly about not discussing the budget in your agreement, modify the first sentence of the example as follows:

My fee for work under this agreement is 30% of all purchases of goods and construction specified for your project by my office.

Of course, the sentence about the retainer should remain. Most designers now insist on retainers or advance fee deposits from clients. Because a large percentage of design time is devoted to early client interviews and preparation of initial plans, money should change hands upon the signing of the agreement. Whatever the fee structure is, don't make the deposit a token amount. Clients can always decide not to continue the project even after preliminary work is done. If an insufficient deposit has not been collected to cover a good portion of time, you will have been working for free.

If you have not estimated the project cost you cannot establish a payment schedule. If you estimate a fee and the project has a certain life, e.g., six months, you can establish a schedule for the client to pay your fee. Of course, if you go over budget with the client's approval, you can bill the additional fees as they are incurred. At least with a schedule, you have set up a basic method of payment.

In the absence of a fixed schedule, you can establish a method for payment as follows:

> My fee for work under this agreement is 30% of all purchases of goods and construction specified for your project by my office. $5,000 is payable upon signing this agreement and shall be nonrefundable. Further, it shall be credited toward subsequent design fees incurred. The balance of my fee shall be billed in conjunction with issuing your purchase orders. Payments for design fees shall be billed as deposits and balances are required by contractors and vendors. In addition, you will receive a monthly statement.

The second paragraph of the cost-plus example has been omitted from this one.

Always state that your design commission is due and payable on all purchase orders that have been approved. Whether the budget has been projected or not, the following sentence is important to your letter:

> In the event during the tenure of this agreement, you determine to discontinue the use of our services on this

project, all commissions will be due and payable with respect to any purchase orders of goods and construction that have been approved by you in writing.

I cannot overemphasize the importance of this. The discussion of your fee has been tied in with fee billing. Fee billing, as the examples illustrate, can be done according to a schedule of payments when there's a budget forecast or in conjunction with purchase orders when a budget isn't mentioned.

Make sure that the client knows that a regular system of billings will be provided by your office. This clause will prevent the loss of commissions on purchases as long as selections have been approved, regardless of delivery, if your client decides to dismiss you in the middle of the project.

If you are charging a fixed or flat fee, state the amount of the design fee and the intervals at which the payments are to be made. In many cases, designers who charge flat fees put in a cut-off date for their services. If the job has not been completed by that date, an additional monthly fee will be imposed. The following is a popular flat-fee clause:

As indicated by our previous consultations and the nature of our services as described earlier in the agreement, a great deal of our design services will be devoted to reworking your existing interior. In view of this, our fee for work under this agreement will be a comprehensive flat fee in the amount of $15,000. It shall be payable as follows:

$2,500	Upon Signing
$2,500	January 1, 1982
$2,500	February 1, 1982
$2,500	March 1, 1982
$2,500	April 1, 1982
$2,500	May 1, 1982.

Each installment when made shall be considered payment for services rendered and shall be nonrefundable. It is contemplated that our work should be completed by June 1, 1982. If you decide to continue to use our services after June 1st, a monthly fee of $1,250 will be required until you feel our design work is complete.

Note that I used the phrase "reworking your existing interior" before leading into the flat fee. Most designers don't charge on a flat fee basis today, especially for residential projects, unless there is a good reason. In this example, the client had used another designer before and was unhappy with the results, not an uncommon situation. The present designer was called in to "rework" the existing interior. Because many important purchases had already been made, it would have been unprofitable to charge work on a retail or cost-plus basis. Remember, when discussing flat fees in your letter, offer some kind of brief rationale to clarify why that method was selected.

The example specifies that each payment is nonrefundable. Also, if the job in question is not completed by June 1st regardless of the reason, the designer will lose money on the project. This clause protects him from any number of variables that could delay the project and keep him working indefinitely without additional compensation. It will also encourage the client to help keep things moving. Any plans of this nature must be clearly spelled out in the letter of agreement. Don't quote a fixed fee without a cutoff date and expect to be paid extra if the job drags on.

In commercial situations, a common method is billing on the basis of the amount of time expended (number of hours) times a multiple.

Direct Personnel Expenses

The following is a clause used by firms who charge on a DPE basis:

> We propose to be compensated for services on a time-card basis at a rate of 2.5 times DPE with a not-to-exceed amount of $20,000. All out-of-pocket expenses for reproductions, travel, postage, messengers, long-distance telephone calls and report typing are to be reimbursed at cost. If inflation continues at its present rate, our firm will increase staff salaries to adjust to cost-of-living increases after four months. This cost-of-living increase would increase the not-to-exceed amount to $23,000.
>
> Direct Personnel Expense is defined as the direct salaries for all our technical personnel engaged on the project and the portion of the cost of their mandatory and customary contributions and benefits related thereto, such as employment taxes, and other statutory employee benefits, insurance, sick leave, holidays, vacations, pensions and similar contributions and benefits.
>
> If after your written approval of documents you wish to

change them for any reason, any additional services required by us for the change will be performed at a rate
of 2.5 times DPE. These are addenda fees, which are in
addition to the base fee.

Most smaller firms will not use the DPE method. However, you should know that it exists and how it works, as
your competition may be using it. It will be more fully discussed in *Charging a Client*. However, there are some
observations to be made from this example. Since charging DPE is a function of hourly time rates, some clients
may get nervous about salary increases over the life of a
project, especially when they are being billed on a multiple.
Therefore, note that this design firm put in an "upset figure" of $23,000. Although the project was not scheduled to
cost that much, at least the client could be certain that the
design fees would not exceed that amount.

Note also that "Direct Personnel Expenses" is defined
directly in the agreement. When charging on this multiple
or any other design multiple, be sure to fully define it in the
agreement. Explaining it orally to the client is generally
insufficient as, in corporate situations, contracts have to
be approved by officers, directors, and other personnel.
Therefore, a commercial agreement should be as
self-explanatory as possible.

It rarely pays for a designer to charge a client on a
straight hourly basis, either commercially or residentially.
Commercial firms usually charge a multiple and make
money. Residential firms are rarely able to convince
clients to pay on a multiple basis so that they generally
don't use an hourly rate.

Another method of charging on a commercial basis is to use a square-footage charge often coupled with a percentage of the project budget. The following is a typical clause for a relatively small commercial project:

> You have advised us that the amount of space to be designed in your office is 10,000 net rentable square feet. Our fee for work under this agreement is as follows:
> $1.50 per square foot for preparation of all construction drawings including cabinet work, elevations, reflected ceiling plans, painting and wall covering schedule, etc., plus ten percent (10%) of the cost of all purchases of goods and construction specified by our office to implement the drawings. A retainer of $7,500 will be due upon signature of the agreement, and another payment of $7,500 is payable upon acceptance of our drawings. The balance of our fees will be billed in conjunction with the issuance of our purchase orders.

Notice that the retainer is one half the cost of preparing the drawings, and the balance of that cost is due upon delivery and acceptance of the drawings. In commercial situations, complete sets of drawings are generally necessary, and the retainer should be one half of the designer's fee for preparing the drawings as specified. The balance should be paid upon delivery, also as specified. The percentage charged for purchases and construction-generally much lower than in residential situations-covers the provision of services for specifications and construction supervision.

This example, if you refer to the example on p.xx, is simply a variation of cost-plus as explained earlier. In fact, an infinite number of variations exist on charging procedures and their presentation in a letter of agreement. Perhaps I have zeroed in on the methods that you use in the previous examples, and you can merely transpose them for your agreements. Most likely, I have not, and you will have your own variations. The important point, however, is that you now know how to structure a discussion of fees in your own letter of agreement.

Disbursements

Always discuss disbursements. If they're not mentioned, many clients assume that all incidental expenses, which can be considerable, are included in the design fee. They may balk later when billed for extra charges if this is not made clear. List all additional charges that are not included in your fee as in the following example:

> In addition to our fee, you shall pay for actual and reasonable disbursements for this project other than normal overhead, including the following: blueprints, reproductions (photostats), messenger service, long-distance phone calls, and local travel expenses. If outside consultants (such as air conditioning, lighting or structural engineers, etc.) are needed, their fees will be paid by client. If, after your written approval of the basic plans, you wish to change them, any additional services required by us for the change will be performed at a rate of $60 per hour. All such disbursements will be billed on a monthly basis,

except for outside consultants, who will only be retained upon your approval.

The first sentence of the example is self-explanatory; these expenses typically occur on all design projects. Outside consultants, however, are an entirely different matter. After you have examined your prospective client's space, you'll have a fairly good idea of whether an outside consultant will be needed. If there is a reasonable chance that one will be required, provide for payment as an additional disbursement. If you know one will not, leave that sentence out of the agreement. It will only confuse and mislead your client.

One of my clients always left in the outside consultants clause in his disbursements section as standard language, whether it was necessary or not, against my advice. A prospective client consulted him for a decorating job, but when she saw that provision, her first reaction was, "What is this designer getting me into? I just want to buy furniture!" After that incident, he only used language when necessary.

The fee for changes in basic plans after a client's written approval must be on a hourly basis. In an interior design project for a residential client, for example, a designer should not prepare construction drawings for cabinets, walls, etc., until after the client approves design sketches. A complete set of drawings, prepared by draftsmen, can cost a great deal. These are then submitted to the client for his written approval. At this stage, the designer should not pay for extensive changes without being reimbursed. Clients have been known to change their mind about everything once a design has been completed. If they do, the designer should be paid for these additional drafting charges, or he'll begin losing money on the project even before he starts to implement the plans.

Some designers use renderings as a visual aid to sell their initial presentation although they are expensive and time consuming. Such designers often stipulate that if additional renderings are requested in the event of extensive design revisions, the client will be billed.

Additional Fees

Clients often change their minds after plans have been finished and purchase orders issued. Suppose a client can't make up her mind about what kind of dining room table she wants. The designer may take her shopping; she'll make a selection; the purchase order will be prepared. Then, she'll call up and cancel—it's not what she really wants. One client "bought" four dining tables before she finally put an order through. The designer complained to me. He was being paid on cost-plus and really went through the effort of purchasing four tables, not one.

To prevent this type of situation, the following clause is used:

> If, after your written approval of purchases of goods and construction, you determine to make substitutions or changes, 30% additional design fee shall be payable on all these approved changes.

Obviously, this is a tough clause to negotiate. I make my clients aware of it but advise them not to use it unless they're ready for opposition. When a prospective client sees this clause, he may think, "Do I have to pay double if I don't buy the first thing he shows me?" In other words, you may be creating suspicion. However, if you don't use this clause and you get a client who cannot make up his mind, you may end up wasting a lot of time without being paid for it if you're charging retail or cost plus.

Payment

If payments are not being made during the project, state that you will stop work until the account is brought up to date, as illustrated by the following example:

> If payment to our office should be withheld longer than fifteen (15) days after billing, we reserve the right to stop progress until such time as remuneration is forthcoming.

Stopping work is one of the most effective ways to make sure you get paid. It's a drastic measure, especially if you're in the middle of supervising construction and your client advises that he is temporarily short of cash. In that case, you will have to decide whether to continue. However, warn your clients about your intentions before you are retained. Then, if payments are withheld, while you are implored to continue, your answer can simply be, "I'm very sorry. It's simply office policy not to work on jobs on which payments are in arrears. That was made clear from the inception of our relationship."

Photographing Privilege

A designer's stock-in-trade is his portfolio and the publicity from his published work. Reserve the right, if possible, to photograph your completed work as illustrated by the following:

> We reserve the right exclusively to photograph our design work after it is completed and to give permission for its use in any publication although your name will not be used without your consent.

Some clients shun publicity and refuse to permit the space to be photographed even when their names are not used. The overwhelming majority, however, will be more than delighted to see their name and environment in print. In fact, the presence of this clause is often impressive. Some clients will be thrilled to think that you can take their space and make it "magazine."

Arbitration

Most businessmen, including interior designers, are faced with either being sued or having to sue someone at least once during their careers. An arbitration clause in a letter of agreement will usually prevent a lawsuit between designer and client. The advantages and disadvantages of arbitration will be discussed in *Avoiding Legal Crises.* Merely keep in mind now that the following clause allows any disputes between you and your client to be settled in an informal, administrative hearing instead of in a courtroom:

> Any dispute or disagreement between parties arising out of or relating to this agreement shall be settled by arbi-

tration in (New York) under the rules then obtaining of the American Arbitration Association and judgment upon the award may be entered in any court having jurisdiction.

Payment Schedule

As I discussed under *Fees*, your client may pay you pursuant to a fixed schedule of payments, depending upon how you charge and the way the agreement is structured.

I have provided a sample payment schedule (See p. 41) that was incorporated into the body of the letter of agreement. Usually, however, payment schedules make up an appendix that requires the client's signature and the date just as the letter of agreement does. The following is an abbreviated schedule:

Schedule of Payments

Upon Signing	$1,500
January 1, 1982	$2,000
February 1, 1982	$2,000
March 1, 1982	$2,000

| Client's Signature | Dated: December 5, 1981 |

| Designer's Signature | Dated: December 5, 1981 |

The amount requested "Upon Signing" is the retainer, which should have been requested earlier in the letter of agreement. The amount does not necessarily have to bear any relationship to the payments themselves. Generally, however, the remaining payments are the same although they can be varied depending upon the situation.

As I have emphasized, once a payment has been made be sure you don't have to refund the money. Your letter should state that each payment, including the retainer, is nonrefundable. On the schedule of payments itself, however, do not insert the word "Nonrefundable." The word appears so glaringly obvious there that I prefer to slip it into the letter during, for example, the discussion of fees.

Closing

Your final paragraph is of the standard type used to conclude a letter of agreement for most purposes. It can vary in style but should contain the following elements:

If the above meets with your approval, your signature below will indicate your acceptance of the terms of the agreement and will indicate your authorization to proceed with work. Kindly return the duplicate copy to us. Of course, if you have any questions, please don't hesitate to call.

We are looking forward to working with you.

Sincerely,

Designer's Name
Design Firm, Inc.

Client's Signature   Dated: January 15, 1982

Send the client two signed copies of the agreement. Although you do not specify in the closing that you won't start the project until you receive the first payment, i.e., the retainer, don't begin work until you have it. If your new client sends back the agreement without the check and then starts calling to make appointments and ask questions, advise him, pleasantly, that you never start projects prior to the receipt of a retainer. Even if you know the check will be sent later on, it is important to set a precedent for prompt payment, particularly at the outset of your relationship.

Conclusion

The letter of agreement is a cornerstone of the client relationship. As the job progresses and difficulties occur, you and your client will refer to it to clarify responsibilities and obligations. Of course, you want to avoid statements that will come back to haunt you, but don't leave gaps or create ambiguities out of fear of putting things in writing. Unfortunately, only personal experience can guide you, but these suggestions will help you along.

As your business evolves and your techniques become more sophisticated, your letter of agreement will change. Even a neophypte should be certain that it is professional.

Charging a Client

A lternative methods of charging a client have already been introduced in Chapter One. Their manner of presentation was discussed in the event the designer had already chosen which method to use. In Chapter Two, I will discuss how to choose a method, the most important issue.

The financial terms, very frequently, will determine whether a client retains a designer or not. Most design firms develop a standard method of charging. However, the circumstances of a prospective job can vary so markedly that one standard rarely can cover all situations. Most prospective clients, especially if a large fee is at stake, will consult with several designers before making a decision. For that reason, your fee must be competitive and your method of charging responsive to the demands of the job.

Keep an open mind. The crucial factor is flexibility. With this caveat, consider this Chapter as a presentation of various points of view, not a presentation of inflexible facts.

Variables Involved

An almost infinite number of variables can influence your decision about which method to use either as a general policy or for specific situations.

The following list is by no means exhaustive but represents a number of these variables:

1. General type of work. Does your firm do more decorating than designing, i.e., specifications of furnishings as opposed to more complex construction through the use of architectural drawings. Designers who perform decorative work for example, tend to charge retail, and designers who perform architectural work frequently charge cost-plus.

2. Type of job. Some specific jobs require more decorating than designing. The same designer might charge retail for a project that would essentially involve purchasing furniture, and he might charge cost-plus for a project using a lot of built-ins requiring contractors and cabinetmakers.

3. Size of job. On very large jobs or commercial jobs, some clients will only pay a pre-set flat fee of a de-escalating percentage of the cost of goods and construction. On smaller jobs, especially residential ones, the percentage can be higher if cost-plus is used. Retail might be selected so that the designer will be paid on an item-by-item basis.

4. Size of design staff. Designers with large offices often charge on a timecard or hourly basis, increased by a multiple such as DPE to insure that they can meet their expenses. Smaller offices sometimes gamble on a larger return by basing their charges upon the size of the expenditures made by their clients by using retail or cost-plus.

5. Credibility of client. Occasionally, a designer will want to undertake a project even if he is unsure as to whether the client will really pay the fee. In that case, he should charge a flat design fee, with a considerable retainer to be collected before starting work. Some designers, on infrequent occasions, have requested the total fee in advance.

6. Residential or commercial project. A decision is often made upon this factor alone. Some designers charge retail for residential projects and cost-plus for commercial projects. There is an increasing tendency to charge cost-plus for residential work today as well, although the percentage for residential on cost-plus is usually much higher than for commercial projects.

7. Project and client variance. Projects and clients can vary so markedly that some designers will not specify how they charge until they receive all the necessary input. The most important factor in a large, commercial project may be the party selected to make the purchases. On a hotel project, for example, if the client uses a purchasing agent instead of the designer, the designer may charge on a flat-fee or monthly basis, especially if he has no role in supervising installations.

8. Consistency. Some designers always charge the same way regardless of the type or size of project. Using one method, they feel, lends credibility and consistency to their image. A uniform method can be easier to operate with and assures prospective clients that they will be offered a standard, fair price. Consistency does help, but no rule requires following one procedure all the time.

9. Combination of methods. Depending upon the situation, designers often combine methods. Some residential designers charge cost-plus on all construction and retail on all purchases. Other designers experiment for years with different combinations until they find the right ones for specific types of projects.

Methods of Charging Design Fees

The following are the methods of charging design fees that are used most frequently and that have worked successfully for my own clients.

Charging Retail

Residential interior decorators have traditionally favored this method, and it still remains extremely popular. Charging retail can encourage clients to use designer services. Clients will feel that money is spent only on goods, as the designer's percentage, which typically ranges from 20 percent to 50 percent, is built-in. In fact, the client is often right. If the merchandise is bought in an open showroom, clients pay only what they would if they bought it themselves without the advice of a designer. Closed showrooms, selling only to the trade, quote only retail to consumers and refuse to reveal wholesale cost, thereby preventing clients from discovering how much the designer's mark-up is.

In the past few years, there has been a tremendous shift away from this method for a number of reasons. Designers no longer feel reluctant to quote a separate design fee because our society is now accustomed to paying fees for endless new services. A designer is now viewed by the vast upper-middle class as necessary in the creation of a home, and, accordingly, design fees have become an accepted expense.

Designers have naturally jumped at the opportunity to

charge a separate design fee so that they can discuss wholesale or net prices with clients. First, it removes an element of secrecy from the designer-client relationship. Many clients paying retail always wanted to know how much something really costs. Now, they know.

As residential designers have become more installation oriented (i.e., budgets are being allocated for cabinet work, sophisticated lighting, mirror work, and other construction), designers can more easily discuss competitive pricing between vendors and contractors with clients when they can talk in net terms.

Retail is now being charged under two general circumstances. The first is a traditional type of residential project, usually involving the purchases of antiques, accessories, lamps, draperies, and fabrics but not much cabinet work, removal of walls, etc. The retail designer largely deals with decorator showrooms and craftsmen, not architects and contractors. The second set of circumstances is when the designer uses a combination method of charging. Cost plus might be charged on all construction and interior architectural expenditures, and retail might be charged for purchasing furniture, fabrics, and accessories.

Charging Cost-Plus

Charging on the basis of a percentage of the wholesale cost of goods and construction (hence cost *plus*) was originally favored by architects. As the interior designer's approach has become more like the architect's, this, in a sense, has become his "modern" method of charging.

The question is, "what percentage?" The range is anywhere from 10 percent to 40 percent. The "10 Percenters" are "housewife decorators" who shop for their neighbors, adding a 10 percent surcharge to all purchases. This is about the lowest figure I am aware of except for tremendous commercial jobs, on which percentages de-escalate to as low as 5 percent once purchases exceed a million dollars.

Most interior designers charge a minimum of 25 percent, at least on the first $50,000 of purchases. Even an office with a relatively low fixed overhead finds this to be the minimum percentage to make a job profitable. In commercial situations, the percentage drops to between 10 and 15, depending upon budget size.

When my residential clients have become fairly successful and can afford to risk losing new business by raising their fees, the first thing they do is increase their percentage to 30. Thirty percent will no longer raise any eyebrows among clients who want one of the well-published residential designers with established reputations. Many famous designers are now charging from 35 percent to 40, and getting it! This league of designers generally uses a project supervisor (i.e., a junior designer) for each client project although the actual design work is done by the firm's principals. These firms often have very high operating overheads because of the many in-house personnel-e.g., draftsmen, senior and junior designers, architects, etc.

Percentages de-escalate quickly for commercial jobs. Interior designers are competing with architects, who traditionally charge lower percentages. Then too, corporate-oriented jobs progress much more quickly. The clients tend to be much more business oriented and unemotional about selections and execution; design decisions move faster.

Residential clients can often take weeks to make up their minds.

Sometimes, designers will charge two percentages for a single commercial job. A common situation would be on a job for several floors of office space. Fifteen percent might be charged for the design of all general office space, including drafting charges, and 25 percent might be charged for heavily designed areas such as main reception areas, the corporate board room, and executive offices. As an across-the-board figure, the highest percentage I am aware of for corporate jobs is 20. High commercial fees are generally charged only when the client wants the space treated in a very customized, residential format.

If a percentage is your sole method of charging (i.e., not coupled with a flat design fee, as will be discussed later), its size should depend upon your competitors' fees, your experience and reputation, office overhead, and the amount of work on hand. Once you set a specific figure, don't change it from one client to the next for jobs in the same category. Designers who have been known to do this lose credibility.

An advantage of this method is the option of using the direct payment technique for purchases. The designer will prepare all the purchase orders with specifications but make the client pay for the goods and services directly. (See Chapter One, *Purchases*). This usually cannot be done when charging retail because the client pays the designer in full as the retail vendor.

Many designers insist that their clients purchase directly (making certain, of course, that they receive wholesale prices) for a number of reasons. First, if the designer makes the purchases as an agent, his clerical work and bookkeeping will be much more involved. Second, if the client cancels a purchase after making the down payment or deposit, the designer will not be caught in the middle as the agent to obtain the payment balance or reclaim the deposit. Third, if defects are discovered in merchandise or construction, the client will look to the vendor or contractor instead of to the designer to make amends.

Some designers find the direct payment method unprofessional. They believe that if they don't make the purchases themselves, they will lose control of the job. Also, because commissions are earned on purchases, they feel a responsibility to maintain their middleman's role in the event of order cancellation or faulty workmanship or materials. However, a designer can still maintain the same supervisory role even if the client makes purchases directly. Legally, he will avoid certain liabilities (to be discussed in *Dealing with Responsibility*), which benefit makes the use of this technique worth considering.

Charging cost-plus has its obvious advantages. The designer receives uniform compensation for all expenditures. With retail, the percentage varies; further, the client may vacillate about his choices because he suspects that his designer will earn more if he buys certain items. Cost-plus eliminates the mystery by full disclosure about all fees.

Charging a Flat Fee

A prearranged fixed fee for creative and supervisory services is the easiest method of charging. When cost-plus or retail is used, the designer is cast in the role of a merchant.

A client realizes that the fee depends upon how much is spent, so sometimes he'll suspect his designer of excessive profit-taking. When clients are so suspicious of their designer and wonder "how much he's going to make off me," the relationship is often doomed.

A flat fee also guarantees the design fee regardless of budget cuts. Occasionally, a client will plan to design an entire residence and later decide that he can't afford it. If a flat fee is used, the designer must be paid even if the client backs out after all the groundwork and conceptual stages have been completed. This approach minimizes a downside risk.

Conversely, this can also work to the designer's disadvantage. If a client *doubles* a budget in the middle of a project, the designer will lose windfall profits that he would have made with retail or cost-plus. For this reason, I usually advise against fixed fees unless there are special circumstances. Most clients usually end up spending more than they intended to, usually not less. That's how designers make more money.

Designers can lose profits on a flat fee if they have to design, redesign, and redesign again. A difficult client who uses up too much design time can cause a real problem. It is generally difficult to renegotiate flat fees once they have been established, so be cautious about quoting a price. Generally, fixed fees work best when a designer knows the client and his behavior pattern. But, then again, you can't really predict how a client is going to act, especially in residential situations, even if you have worked with him previously.

There is one safety valve for flat fees as mentioned in

Chapter One, *Fees*. A final cut-off date should be stipulated for rendering services at the specified fee. After that date, an additional fee can be imposed on a time basis, i.e., usually monthly. If, for example, a project is not completed in six months, regardless of the reason, and services were to be provided for that period for $15,000 ($2,500 per month), an additional monthly fee of $1,500 might be charged until the designer's work is finished.

A cut-off date helps bring a job to an end. It urges the client to encourage completion instead of prolonging the project with changes, delays, and indecisiveness. Clients are so anxious to avoid paying design fees that they will act expeditiously in order to finish as soon as possible. Of course, if at the end of the six-month period, a designer needs only to supervise late deliveries and other odds-and-ends, he won't charge any extra.

The imposition of additional charges after the cut-off date requires careful consideration. In the example, six months was enough to complete the project. The designer was very careful not to shortchange the client for the flat fee. As the period was generous, the additional monthly charge was only 60 percent as much as the initial monthly charge. As a rule-of-thumb, additional monthly charges are approximately 50 percent of the initial monthly charges when the initial fee is large enough and prorated monthly.

It's difficult to tell a designer how to set a flat fee, and the whole process generally makes designers insecure. Too high a figure might scare the client away, but a too low one will not be profitable. One intangible, of course, is the client. If the job looks smooth and the client amiable, the designer doesn't have to worry as much about getting rid of the project for a specified number of dollars.

There are two basic methods of setting flat fees. The first is to estimate the size of the budget once the scope of the project is clear and determine how large the design fee would be if cost-plus were being charged. The second is to estimate the amount of time the project will require and place a price tag on the value of the services.

Try using both methods on the same project when setting your own flat fee and see how closely the figures coincide. Comparisons of this sort can help act as a system of checks and balances.

Surprisingly, some of my most successful clients never use specific methods when deliberating on the size of a flat fee. They have the experience to assess a project and say, "This is the amount the job is worth and that's how much I want to do it." These designers have worked on analogous situations before, and they can come to rapid conclusions. I always advise designers with less experience to avoid using flat fees unless there is some compelling reason.

Charging by the Hour

The concept of residential designers being compensated on a straight hourly basis has never appealed to my clients. Interior design for individual residences is not a mechanical process, and, accordingly, charging mechanically by the hour rarely provides sufficient compensation.

Most designers are more flexible about charging by the hour for commercial work. Commercial design generally has a different point of view, and clients approach it from a more practical perspective. However, a straight hourly fee is usually increased by a multiple (See Chapter One, *Fees*), such as DPE, which is frequently 2.5. A large interior design firm can justify a multiple in terms of hiring personnel and paying for overhead. Smaller firms cannot generally persuade their clients to go along with this procedure and have to charge a straight hourly amount. The range for designers and their employees generally falls between $30 and $100 per hour.

Most residential designers who charge by the hour use a straight hourly rate, which generally approximates $50 per hour. However, the total design fee usually ends up as substantially less than if another method had been selected.

Charging an Intitial Design Fee

An initial design fee, payable upon signature of the letter of agreement, can be used when charging retail or, more frequently, cost-plus. Don't confuse this fee with a retainer, which can also be used with cost-plus. A retainer is an initial payment as well but serves as an advance against future commissions. It is credited after design commissions have accrued.

A design fee is *in addition* to commissions charged using cost-plus or mark-ups received when charging retail. It is not credited against any subsequent fees.

The following are typical examples of when an initial design fee might be used.

1. *Charging retail when designing a four-room apartment.* A design fee of $500 per room (i.e., $2,000) is requested on signature of the letter of agreement. If the designer completes floor plans and furniture layouts but the client decides not to continue with the project or make any purchases, the design fee will be some compensation for the initial design work.

2. *Charging cost-plus when designing a four-room apartment.* The initial budget is projected at $40,000. A design fee of $4,000 is requested on signature of the letter of agreement. The percentage on purchases of goods and construction is 20 percent. Again, the design fee acts as compensatory protection if the client doesn't follow through on the project. If the project is completed, the designer's fee will be a total of $12,000-30 percent of overall budget. If the designer normally charges 30 percent and the client goes over the budget, the designer would have done better to have waived a design fee and charged 30 percent across the board. However, the design fee was a good way of hedging the fee in the event the client did not complete the job.

3. *Charging Cost-Plus when designing the interior of a large residence or commercial structure and working with architects and builders.* On a project of this nature, a design fee works best when the job is divided into phases.

A three-phase structure as illustrated by the following sample letter of agreement will show how an initial design fee can be divided into payments and used with cost-plus.

Our services to design your residence will be divided into three phases as follows:

Phase One: Consultant to the Architects, Builders, Landscape Architects and Exterior Lighting Experts.

For all the design areas, we will supply the architect and general contractor with architectural drawings for the following:
1. Siting of house and terraces
2. Facades and roof
3. Exterior stone work
4. Entrance doors and hardware
5. Plumbing, including fixtures and appliance selections
6. Reflected ceiling plan
7. Exterior painting schedule
8. Other necessary specifications with respect to exterior decor

As compensation for these services, our fee of $60,000 shall be payable as follows:

$20,000 Upon signing this Letter of Agreement,
$20,000 Upon completion and acceptance of plans, drawings, and specifications.
$20,000 Upon completion of Phase I.

Upon completion of our services for Phase I, we will commence the second phase.

Phase Two: Interior Finishes and Built-Ins.

We will supply specifications and prepare purchase orders, where necessary, for the following:

- Decorative hard surface floor coverings
- Boiseries
- Decorative plasterwork
- Interior painting
- Marble work
- Fireplaces
- Mirror and metal work
- Decorative hardware
- Tile and millwork

As compensation for our services, we will submit estimates based upon our cost plus 20 percent.
As the second phase progresses, we shall undertake the third phase as it becomes appropriate.

Phase Three: Furnishings and Decorative Items.

We will supply specifications and prepare purchase orders, where necessary, for the following:

- Wallcoverings
- Rugs and carpeting
- Window treatments
- Custom-made furniture
- Lighting fixtures
- Accessories
- Outdoor furniture
- Other necessary items to complete furnishing

As compensation for our services, we will submit estimates based upon our cost plus 30 percent.

If you request that we select antiques, works of art, and objects d'art, you will be charged a 10 percent commission above our cost.

We would also be happy to assist you to advise on the selection of china, glassware, flatware, linens, etc., through our own sources and request a service fee of 10 percent above our cost.

This example illustrates the use of a fixed fee with three other percentages for charging cost-plus. The initial design fee of $60,000 was based on a construction estimate between $750,000 and $1,000,000, therefore, less than 10 percent. Receiving 20 percent on finishes and 30 percent on furnishings for a project of this size enabled the initial design fee to be set so low.

Initial design fees are tremendously valuable in such large projects, as the one in the example when they are well thought out. They should cover a large portion of the initial design services, but should not be too high, especially if the percentage for making all interior purchases is 25 percent or more.

This discussion on how to charge has not been meant as an exhaustive treatment. Designers always tell me about methods that they have invented that work for their own business. There should be no hard and fixed rules about how to charge; however, the methods discussed here are the ones which, in my experience, operate the most efficiently and have been accepted by the public.

CHAPTER THREE

Dealing with Responsibility

The implementation and execution of design plans by the interior designer places him in the center of a huge web of responsibilities. If the designer doesn't know how to handle them, obligations, duties, and responsibilities can become hopelessly entangled.

This chapter is divided into a number of segments defining areas of responsibility. Managing them well is the mark of a successful designer. Some of my most talented and creative clients are doomed to obscure careers of financial mediocrity because they refuse to master the facets of their business. Once the designer is able to recognize "who he is" and "where he is," then he will be able to perform at the necessary levels.

Avoiding a Legal Crisis

A designer often becomes involved in a lawsuit because of a failure in his client relationship. It may not be the designer's fault at the time, and it happens to some of the best. However, because legal action is an unfavorable outcome, let's discuss this first to illustrate the terrible problem of having to settle conflicts in the courts.

Obviously, the best way to handle a legal crisis is to avoid one. Unfortunately, this is not always possible, and sometimes the designer must utilize legal means to protect himself and get paid.

Although certain client disputes cannot be settled without the involvement of a third party, many interior designers who have sued to collect fees are overwhelmed by the trauma and financial expense from lawsuits. For that reason, as I have already mentioned, I always ask my clients to consider arbitration as an alternative to litigation.

Here is a good illustration of why going to court to collect unpaid fees is not always successful:

> A residential designer in Los Angeles completed a $300,000 project for a client who owed him a balance of $12,000 in design fees. When the client refused to pay any of it, the designer made unsuccessful attempts to collect with letters and telephone calls and finally retained an attorney to start a lawsuit. After six weeks of serving legal papers and answering pre-trial motions made by the client's attorney, the case went to trial. The designer lost two days in court and ended up settling for $9,000. He had to pay a legal fee, one third of the recovery ($3,000) and some court costs. He ended up with about $5,500, less than half of what he was owed. The designer realized that this process was too expensive and time consuming even though he had "won."

When this designer asked me to prepare a letter of agreement for a different client, I advised that another vehicle exists which is designed to settle differences faster than a court and, accordingly, to save on legal fees. It's called *arbitration*.

Arbitration is a legal alternative for resolving disputes without going to court. The American Arbitration Association (AAA), is a not-for-profit public service organization that provides private settlement dispute services.

Arbitration can be voluntary, and its use depends upon the agreement of both parties. However, when I have represented plaintiffs in disputes and asked the opposition to submit to arbitration, generally there was resistance, and I had to go to court. But if there is an arbitration clause in your contract, the matter will automatically go to arbitration for settlement.

As mentioned in Chapter One, the AAA has developed a standard arbitration clause that can be inserted in your letter of agreement as follows:

Any claim or controversy arising out of or relating to this contract, or the breach thereof, shall be settled by arbitration in accordance with the Rules of the American Arbitration Association, and judgment upon the award rendered by the arbitrator(s) may be entered in any Court having jurisdiction thereof.

There is one important point to make clear. Prior to inserting this clause or any other clauses in your letter of agreement, check with your lawyer. He will undoubtedly be familiar with AAA, which has 24 regional offices and more than 50,000 impartial arbitrators. He will tell you how or if this clause should be modified and whether arbitration is a good method for you to use in general or in a specific situation. Any further questions about arbitration can probably be answered by the AAA.

You are not required to use a lawyer when you go to arbitration. If the amount in dispute is substantial, it's always safer to use a good attorney. Nonetheless, I have found that because arbitration takes less time than most legal actions, fees are lower than for a conventional lawsuit. When the AAA arbitrates, there is an administrative fee of 3 percent for up to $10,000 of the claim, with a $150 minimum. For disputes ranging from $10,000 to $25,000, the fee is $300 plus 2 percent of the excess over $10,000. However, these fees must be wieghed against court costs, which can also be substantial.

The AAA supplies attorneys with a set of forms, and starting the procedure is generally less involved than commencing a legal action. Usually, only one hearing is held before a selected arbitrator, thus eliminating pre-trial motions and pre-trial depositions (hearings without a judge), which are often held prior to an ordinary trial. Also, a typical legal action requires a pre-trial conference and then a trial on a different day.

Unless your arbitration clause specifies otherwise, the hearing will most likely be held before one arbitrator. This arbitrator does not have to be a judge and sometimes is not even a lawyer. The AAA will send both parties a list of potential arbitrators and their qualifications for mutual selection. One hopes that someone with experience in the field of design might be picked. If you or your opponent does not like the choice for a good reason, generally you can choose another arbitrator.

Both sides are given a choice of dates for the hearing, and the AAA has always been very lenient when I have requested adjournments. On the hearing date, both parties come with their witnesses and documents that substantiate their claims. If your opponent wants to impose a counterclaim against you that relates to the initial claim, he is entitled to do so in the original set of arbitration petitions; you are permitted to respond at the hearing.

The hearing itself is generally held on an informal basis. As it is an administrative procedure as opposed to a court procedure, the rules of evidence are generally not enforced. The party who commences the action presents his case first, and all documents, statements, and witnesses are presented by his attorney. The arbitrator will often ask questions to clarify any ambiguities. When this phase is complete, the other side will present its defense and related counterclaims with oral and written evidence.

The lack of formality makes participants more relaxed in this type of hearing because they are able to understand what is happening. However, sometimes this absence of formality permits a release of hostilities, and the parties start arguing. Arbitrators are not too pleased with this kind of behavior, so try always to keep control.

Most hearings I have participated in have taken less than a day. However, if the situation is very complicated and a lot of witnesses are needed, hearings will continue until both parties and the arbitrator are satisfied that the case is fully heard. Both parties can produce all the documents and witnesses that they feel are necessary to prove their case within reason. And, as in a court of law, all testimony is made under oath.

Once the hearing is finished, the arbitrator will make his decision and grant an award promptly if not necessarily on the same day. This award is usually final and binding. If the party who is supposed to pay doesn't, the award is enforceable in a court of law. Moreover, it rarely is possible to make an appeal. Once the award is made, that's it.

If you are a winner, all is well. You don't have to wait months for your money and pay more legal fees while an appeal is pending. But if you are a loser, there is generally no right to appeal in a court of law, and you will be compelled to comply with the terms of the award.

An arbitration clause itself can be a great tactical advantage to an individual interior designer or small design firm. Often wealthy clients have a business and pay for legal help on a retainer basis. They can realize that if their designer starts an ordinary lawsuit, the designer will probably lose a lot more time, energy and money than they will. If they have a large legal arsenal at their disposal, their attorneys might be instructed to drag out the whole affair to induce either a small settlement or the discontinuance of the action.

For example, if you have a claim against a client and your attorney will not take the case on a contingency basis (i.e., a fee based on the percentage of the amount collected), you may be unable to afford to pursue the matter. But an arbitration clause decreases the risk of a protracted proceeding. Your client will be aware of this, which may, in turn, affect his judgment. The presence of an arbitration clause increases the odds of private settlement before a proceeding is even started. Without the clause, a wealthy business client may say, "Let him send me a summons and see what happens."

While all this sounds very favorable, some of my clients still don't like arbitration. They feel that a court of law is the most effective forum for their claims and that the threat of a legal action is a more menacing weapon. It's best usually to put the clause in the letter of agreement and wait until something happens. If the matter goes to arbitration, you will see all the pros and cons of arbitration on a firsthand basis. If you like the approach, continue to use the clause. If not, omit it from all future contracts.

Of course you can always run your projects in such a professional way so that neither arbitration or lawsuits are necessary. More in-depth discussion of designer-client relationships follows in this Chapter, but now re-examine the example on page 74 in this part.

Although all the details are not provided in the example, the situation was a very bewildering one. I couldn't understand why the designer had permitted his client to get so behind on fees. Even on large jobs, designers must keep their billing and collections up to date. Most letters of agreement should provide that if bills are not paid within fifteen days after their receipt, the designer will stop all work on the project (Chapter One). And most of them do just that. Of course, there are extenuating circumstances, and exceptions should sometimes be made. However, $12,000 of arrears is a serious matter even in a project of that budget size. Monitor your contract and billing procedures to prevent this kind of situation and legal crisis from arising.

Of the numerous other ways to avoid litigation, preventative measures are always the best and generally the cheapest. Be sure that the right party is signing the agreement, especially in commercial situations, as illustrated by the following:

A designer with a new office in the New York City area was consulted about a substantial commercial job. His letter of agreement was returned with the signature of a ranking employee of the business. He wanted to return the agreement to the owner of the business for his own signature on the grounds that the arrangement was made on a personal basis. Before sending it, the designer checked with me to see if he was being "too cautious."

I told him to stick to his plan. His decision to obtain a binding signature was correct. Although such action may have not been absolutely necessary from a legal standpoint, his logic and instincts were practical and sensible.

When you enter a relationship with a new client, problems may arise that will be difficult to resolve. So it is better to eliminate this particular potential problem now with a letter or telephone call. Unless a client is trying to avoid responsibility at a later date by having an unauthorized employee execute the agreement, he cannot reasonably object to signing properly. Therefore, if a client still refuses to sign the contract after a detailed explanation, you should probably forego the entire project.

Legally, however, the signature of a "ranking employee" may be adequate to bind a client, depending upon the position of the ranking employee in the client's company and the organization of the business itself.

When dealing with a partnership, you are wise to obtain

the signatures of all the general partners. In many states, if the partnership defaults, the general partners will be personally responsible for compliance with the terms of the agreement.

A corporation's liability is generally limited to the assets of the company itself. Accordingly, when doing business with a corporation, bind the corporate entity unless you can get a personal guarantee from officers or shareholders. Personal guarantees are not usually requested or generally given for designer contracts, unless the company is new or its financial situation appears to be shaky. Also, a request of this nature often hinges upon the balance of power in an existing designer-client relationship. If, for example, the designer is well known, with a good reputation and plenty of clients, and the client is a small, obscure concern, the request for a personal guarantee might be delivered as a polite ultimatum. On the other hand, if the designer needs the business and the corporate client appears solid after some investigation, the request should be made gingerly, if at all.

Corporate officers are usually empowered to execute agreements that bind their company. Ranking employees in large corporations are sometimes authorized to enter into agreements as well. For example, the officers of major corporations would not necessarily sign a designer contract to renovate three floors of office space. In this situation, the designer might send a memorandum to the president requesting execution by an officer. If company rules and procedures dictate delegation of authority, your memorandum in conjunction with the response issued by the officer to the designer will most likely bind the company.

On the other hand, if you are designing the same space for a small, recently organized corporation, perhaps you should accept only the president's signature.

If a contract is executed by a ranking employee who is not authorized to sign agreements, all is not necessarily lost. For example, if the company treasurer signs a retainer check as initial payment for a design fee and subsequently initials presentation sketches or working drawings and purchase orders, these acts may "ratify" the initial agreement, subsequently binding the corporation to its entire terms. Or if the corporate president advises in a memorandum that the ranking employee had the authority to execute the contract, his delegation of responsibility may clothe the ranking employee with sufficient authority to bind the corporation. However, delegation of authority to an employee should be established in writing. Oral assurances by company executives or other personnel may give the employee apparent authority, but this may be very difficult to prove in the absence of written documentation.

As a practical matter, however, it is best to rely on legal means to enforce an agreement in a court or arbitration proceeding. These proceedings can be expensive, time consuming and energy draining. The purpose of this chapter, in fact, is to point out how to avoid litigation. It is always smart to quietly investigate the solvency of small corporate clients in particular and to be conservative if the question of authority arises.

In summary, three preventative measures should be taken to avoid a legal crisis:

1. Provide an arbitration clause in the letter of agreement.
2. Keep client billings and collections up to date.
3. Be sure the right party executes the letter of agreement.

Running a Project with Other Design Professionals

The interior designer is rarely in trouble when he is the sole professional on a design project. He is the center of the operation and gives all the orders. But when the designer is hired in conjunction with other design professionals for a single project, architects, engineers, general contractors, and other consultants will all have their own ideas about their responsibilities, boundaries, and limitations.

Unfortunately, the interior designer often winds up on the defensive for one reason: His profession is the newest on the design scene. Architects and engineers have their traditional roles and areas of responsibility. The job of the interior designer is often not as clearly defined. It may seem to him that architects often only relinquish to him those tasks that they reject. He must often fight to define and defend his own design territory.

These conflicts manifest themselves in many different areas. Two common problems occur—during the project planning phase, when architects, contractors, engineers, etc., meet with the client to discuss plans, preliminary budgets, and fees, and during the construction phase—after the drawings are completed and construction is in progress. During project planning, a conflict over fees often arises as will be illustrated by the following example. This initial planning stage, during which the designer establishes his rapport with the client and other professionals, is perhaps the most important phase for him. It sets the stage for the remainder of the project. Running the project with precision at this point is crucial.

> A residential designer in the San Francisco area consulted me during project planning with a client who wanted to build a huge, expensive house. An architect had already been engaged, and discussions were also being held with a general contractor and several consulting engineers. The designer planned to charge using his usual method, cost plus 30 percent. The architect charged cost plus 15 percent, and the designer was concerned about specifying materials for the interior and seeing the architect get paid for his efforts.

I told the designer that his concern was justified and that negotiations with the client and the architect had to be handled very delicately until his letter of agreement had been signed.

This situation is becoming very typical. Until the 1960's, an interior designer was rarely asked to help plan the space for a new commercial or residential structure. Architects generally prempted that role. They designed the space from the outside in. When they finished, the designer was hired. Generally, there wasn't much left to "design." Construction was finished, and, basically, the designer had only to decorate the space with furniture, accessories, floor and wall coverings, etc.

Things have changed a great deal. Some of the spaces created by great architects are uncomfortable and inhuman. Sophisticated clients begin consulting an interior designer before approving their architect's plans. Spaces are now designed from the inside out.

Architects, in many cases, have preferred to isolate themselves from interior designers. Some want designers excluded from initial planning stages. In every respect, interior designers must use affirmative measures to defend their vantage points. When design fees are involved, one must begin in the letter of agreement. This, of course, takes place during the project planning phase.

I advised my client to go through this phase without preparing any sketches or drawings and negotiate his letter of agreement simultaneously. He attended joint meetings with the client, architect, and several contractors, never mentioning the subject of fees. He simply conducted himself as if he had already been hired. After the client had been impressed with the way that the designer integrated himself into the project, the designer met with him separately to discuss the letter of agreement.

If a designer is charging a flat fee, an hourly fee, or any type of time-based fee, obviously there is no problem. Compensation is totally independent of any third-party relationships, i.e., with architects, contractors, or engineers. However, because the trend today is to charge cost-plus, this designer had to explain to his prospective client what belonged in his budget.

In an analogous situation, you might have to do the same. The client must be advised orally, as well in the letter of agreement (See Chapter One), about what belongs in his budget. This should be done as early in the project as possible.

Explain that all items specified by you are included in the budget for commission purposes. This rule of thumb is the easiest way to define your territory. All specifications should be documented by a purchase order and signed by the client. To prevent misunderstandings, put these provisions in your letter of agreement. (See Chapter One, *Includable Items*.) Specifically list items, e.g., custom plumbing and hardware fixtures, lighting and switching, wall coverings and interior painting schedule, window treatments, flooring and floor coverings, and cabinet work.

It's obvious how this might operate for your benefit. Take the master bathroom for example. You might be called upon to create a special bath with custom fixtures. If you provide the interior architectural drawings and specify the fixtures, those expenditures should be incorporated into the interior design budget for commission purposes.

This is an easy situation. A more difficult one might relate to "flooring and floor coverings." Suppose, for example, that the architect specifies hardwood floors for the entire residence and the client approves. Obviously, the cost of installing those floors will not be in your budget. However, a "one-floor treatment" is rarely the pattern for an expensive residence. Marble or slate could be used in the foyer or dining room; carpeting might go in the bedroom. These choices are generally made by the client and the interior designer. The cost of "custom choices" should be included in your budget.

The same logic applies to wall coverings and interior painting. The interior designer selects custom wall coverings and makes selections for custom colors. The material and labor costs necessary to implement these design decisions also belong in the designer's budget.

One other item that should be included is cabinet work. If the architect supplies the drawings for the kitchen cabinets, that will be included in his budget. If the client wants you to design the kitchen, i.e., either by preparing your own drawings for custom work or purchasing cabinets from a specialty manufacturer, this cost should be incorporated in your budget. Generally, all custom bathroom vanities, dining room cabinetry, bookshelves, and banquette seating etc., are custom cabinet items created by the interior designer, not the architect. Make sure they are listed in your letter of agreement under "cabinet work."

All these items are fairly expensive. If you can convince your client to pay for your selections for those categories, you will have a large budget and earn a substantial commission on an expensive, custom-built residence. One way to induce a client to do this is to offer certain services at "no charge." State these gratuities in your letter of agreement immediately after you have specified what will be included in your budget. For example, you could act as a consultant for exterior architectural materials. Because the exterior must complement the interior, it's only logical to extend yourself in this area. You could also offer your services for landscaping and the pool area. If the architect keeps you out of that decision-making process, at least you have made the offer, and your goodwill looks convincing.

If you consult for "no charge" on pool areas, terraces, and gardens, you should still charge if you select any furniture or furnishings for these areas. Accordingly, when you list the areas included in your budget, add "outdoor furniture."

All this free advice, of course, is optional. The project may be so difficult that you will only do architectural consultation for an additional hourly charge. If that's the case, tell your client and so indicate in your letter of agreement. If you don't do this, your client will probably expect you to provide this consultation without charge anyway.

Items generally excluded from the interior designer's budget include stereo equipment, burglar alarms, fire detectors, and intercoms. However, if you design cabinets to house this equipment, the cabinet work itself should be included.

In the example on p. 84, the architect's percentage is one half of the interior designer's with regard to the cost plus percentage. This is frequently the case, as the architect's budget is often two and three times higher than the interior designer's. Many clients, of course, prefer to put as many items in the architect's budget as possible in order to pay a lower percentage in fees and want the interior designer to include his services for nothing. Be prepared for this attitude.

Often the client will have private discussions of your fees with the architect and the general contractor in order to find out the "usual practice." If the architect or contractor wants to discuss your contract or budget, simply refuse. Your relationship with your client is confidential. Don't answer to any third parties for any reason. If the client advises you that he has "surveyed the situation and finds your fees overreaching," merely say that this is your system and, if it would reassure him, he should check with other designers.

Of course, you can always compromise if you're getting close to signing your contract. For example, you could offer not to bill your percentage against a dining room chandelier, a coffee table, or some other token luxury item. That is simply good business sense if the fee warrants it.

It doesn't pay to give in too much. Advise your clients that although you will provide certain services gratuitous- . ly, you will not advise in major areas of decision making for the interior if those items are not included in your budget. Clarify your role at the outset to insure payment.

A conflict over design responsibility often arises in the construction phase as illustrated by the following:

An interior designer in New York City who had been renovating a Manhattan townhouse with an architect, consulting engineer, and general contractor consulted me. He said that the architect and contractor had tried to ignore his design input as much as possible, but that the client instructed them to work with him and utilize his interior construction and cabinet drawings. The designer had been extremely diligent and had supervised construction by the subcontractors at the project site whenever possible. The first real problem arose upon inspection of the kitchen and bathroom. The designer's specifications had been changed without his consultation or approval. The fixtures were in different areas, and the cabinet work details were altered. The designer reported this immediately to his client, who called the contractor and architect. They said that the changes were necessary because the designer's drawings were inadequate. Neither of them had even mentioned any problem with the drawings before.

There is no single solution to this predictable sort of problem. The situation is an extreme example of the poorest sort of working relationship of an architect, contractor, and interior designer. The architect and contractor openly resisted working with the interior designer. They changed his drawings without his approval, and when construction errors were made, they attempted to shift the responsibility and blame to him.

There is one easy and very effective way to prevent this problem from arising. A number of my clients, established designers with excellent reputations, refuse to work on a project unless the client will select a contractor from their list. This is a very restrictive condition to impose. Clients usually reserve the option to select their own contractors when plans are sent out for competitive bids.

I was once instructed by a designer to specify the name of a particular contractor in a letter of agreement for a prospective client. I suggested leaving the decision up to the new client.

"Absolutely not!" the designer protested emphatically. "My cabinet work has very special detail. One contractor understands my work and gets it finished at budget and on schedule. If I can't work with him I'll let the client go. It's not worth it. I'm not going to try to educate a new contractor to the way I design, especially with an architect looking over his shoulder."

Although controlling the selection of a contractor or subcontractors is ideal, it is hardly realistic. Most designers would lose prospective clients if they insisted on making their own choices. The interior designer generally must adapt to the contractor, not vice versa.

Fortunately, the circumstances in the example are unusual. The responsibility for supervision of subcontractors on the site of a project frequently overlaps among the architect, general contractor, and interior designer. Among professionals, precise delineation of duties among professionals may not be terribly important so long as there are no personality conflicts or costly construction mistakes. In the example, both adverse elements are present.

If it becomes clear during the construction phase, that the architect or contractor will be hostile, stay very close to your client. Once your construction drawings are complete, deliver a copy of the plans to the architect. Indicate in a covering letter that you would be willing to make any necessary changes. Send a copy of the letter to your client. If the architect finds fault with your drawings at some subsequent time (as in the example), it will be easy to prove to your client that you gave the architect sufficient opportunity to make changes with your assistance. You will have put him on his guard. Chances are, the architect will recognize this, and be cautious about making modifications without first consulting you.

Once your plans have been submitted and all changes have been made, make sure your client signs the drawings. Then, submit them to the contractor(s) with the architect's plans for competitive bidding. Because drawings must be precise, indicate on each one, "Spotcheck field dimensions." Once the contractor is selected, send him a letter requesting any comments if he feels changes or interpretations are necessary. Send a copy of this correspondence to your client as well.

When construction starts on the interior, visit the site as frequently as possible. Make sure the contractor is following your drawings. The quality and supervision of the work are his responsibility. If there is anything wrong, make notes and report to your client immediately.

If the designer in the example had followed all these precautions, he could not have been held responsible for sanctioning unauthorized changes. They would have been the fault of the architect or contractor. If the client blamed the designer, he could have replied, "These mistakes aren't my fault. I prepared the original plans. First, they were submitted to the architect. He approved them. Then, you signed them. Finally, the drawings were sent to the contractor. You have a copy of my correspondence. He had every opportunity to make changes, but didn't. I watched construction carefully. As soon as I saw the changes, I notified you at once." With that type of procedure, you will avoid being held responsible for the mistakes or interference of others. Your professional responsibility will have been discharged at every juncture.

This strategy is basically defensive. A better way to handle the situation is to be "offensive" with an architect and a contractor. Once your initial plans and your material selections have been completed, call a meeting of the architect, contractor, and client at your office, i.e., your own territory.

Review the plans carefully. Make sure your client pays

attention, participates, and expresses his approval to the others. In effect, you must state to the architect and contractor, "Here are my plans. This is what the client wants. He has approved my ideas in front of all of us. If you can't use them or want to make important changes, you better say so-now." Of course, this doesn't mean that the architect and contractor must make all revisions at that moment. But if they don't forcefully object to your design approach and plans or state emphatically that the drawings will have to be redone, it will be much more awkward for them to make major changes in your work later on.

Thus far, I have discussed the responsibility of the interior designer to use a careful approach to insure the proper implementation of his own design plans. He must somehow delegate some of this responsibility for execution to the architect and the general contractor. It will take teamwork among the three of them to get his plans realized.

There is another area in which the interior designer must maintain his ascendance: the taste level of the completed project. Why? Generally, any client who hires an interior designer at the very outset of a design project involving exterior construction is fairly sophisticated. He will probably want the space to be designed for comfort and warmth, and desires his architect to be guided so that the interior will reflect his lifestyle. Architects may often overlook or neglect these aspects.

The interior designer must involve himself in as many material selection phases as possible. For example, he should act as a consultant for exterior architectural materials, which should obviously complement the color schemes for the interior. General landscaping, pools, terraces, and gardens are other areas about which designers should advise.

If an architect objects to your "interference," merely note that the project must be designed from the "inside out" as well as from the "outside in." For example, the designer typically selects all outdoor furniture for all "outdoor living areas." It certainly follows that he should be an adjunct consultant for architectural materials as well.

Watch your client's reactions when you are expressing your own opinions during this process. He'll appreciate your efforts on his behalf.

All too often the architect and contractor lose sight of what the client wants during a design project. They want to complete the project according to their own specifications. The interior designer must insure that the results suit the client's needs. The designer's success, in most cases, hinges upon how diplomatic he is able to be with other professionals. Sometimes, as in the example, the architect and contractor may be impossible to handle and even unite against him. Usually the case is not so dire, and how well the designer is received depends largely on his client's support and his own tact.

All this expertise on the designer's part requires many hours of consultation. It is much easier to decorate a space after it has been constructed than to participate in planning of the construction during each project phase. As has been discussed, you must structure your letter of agreement so as to be properly compensated for these extra efforts. If your requests are reasonable and your client really wants your assistance at all levels of the project's phases, he'll agree to pay you for these additional services.

The interior designer is one of the newest professionals in the design field. Working with others on a project, defining his role, determining his fees and his areas of authority and responsibility—all these are gray areas for the designer. The burden rests on this generation of designers to clarify, define, and illuminate.

Balancing Responsibilities to Clients and Vendors

Two of the most important assets an interior designer has are his clients and vendors. It's obvious why the client is so important. Without clients, there is no business. Vendors, in some cases, can even be more important than specific clients. Designers usually use the same ones for many jobs and would be hard pressed to replace them. Most designers find themselves constantly tested in regard to their responsibilities to both parties. In some cases, the designer gets caught in the middle between the client and the vendor.

The initial problem of a designer in regard to clients usually relates to the project budget. The budget has always been a sticky problem. Some clients want to know how much they have to spend even before they decide what they want. Most designers try to be honest, but they are naturally hesitant to commit themselves to hard figures until they have been hired and are well into the project. The following is a typical situation in which a designer had been asked to project costs in writing before being retained:

An interior designer in New York was consulted by a prospective client to redesign a two-bedroom apartment. The space was to be entirely refurnished, and a certain amount of built-in cabinet work was required. This was the client's first attempt at entirely redesigning his home. After the designer had been thoroughly interviewed in a number of meetings, he was asked to provide a letter of agreement. The contract explained that the design fee would be based upon a percentage of goods and services purchased to implement the design, i.e., cost-plus. After receiving the agreement, the client called the designer and asked him to insert a budget figure. The designer hesitated to do this, not being certain how much his client really wanted to spend and not wanting to quote a definite price. After finally estimating a budget, the designer consulted me to find out if he would be legally responsible for completing the job for that amount.

I advised that discussing the budget with a client is a very sensitive issue and must be handled with care. The majority of clients are very dollar conscious and if they think that their designer is not, chances are that they will look elsewhere.

In this situation, the client wanted to know from the outset how much he was going to have to spend. Such a figure is difficult, if not impossible, to state exactly even if all requirements and preferences are known from the beginning. As this client was unsure of himself, he wasn't sure how far he wanted to go in one of the most expensive design areas—custom cabinet work. Also, the client hadn't fully revealed what his needs were or how much he would be willing to spend.

There are several approaches to this problem, any one of which may allay a client's fears and enable him to trust you.

Most designers spend a considerable time being interviewed by a client before they are retained. Even those with prestigious reputations must often go through this exercise. Although this is a tedious and time-consuming process, the "getting-acquainted" period can be essential to the establishing of useful parameters once the job commences.

These interviews and the time they require are all part of the "cost of doing business' and should be viewed as any other overhead expense—i.e., office rent, staff salaries, etc. Some designers estimate that they are retained by three out of every ten clients who consult them, and large commercial firms often report a ratio as low as one in ten.

During these interviews, the designer is generally shown the space and questioned about his ideas. He should present his portfolio to illustrate how he has treated similar spaces. Often, a client will look at a project and say, "I like that. Can you create that feeling for me?" If that is the case, the designer will know what this client is looking for and can at least have a "ballpark" figure as to how much it will cost to design the new space with a similar design approach.

During these interviews the designer should question his client as to whether he intends to keep any of his existing furniture and accessories. If so, the designer should deduct these items from his budget and make an inventory of those possessions that will be used on the project.

Once all the initial exploration is completed, the designer then can make a projected estimate. For example, if a client wants a living room with new, contemporary furniture, new carpeting, painting, and light fixtures, many designers will state a minimum cost of $25,000. Orally, the figure may be itemized by quoting general prices for painting, carpentry, floor covering, upholstery, etc.

Given the preceding example, it would be wise to insert the following sentence in your letter of agreement: "Based upon our discussion, the projected estimate for designing your living room will be $25,000." When your client receives the letter, the figure will come as no surprise. You have already discussed general costs with him in depth, and, if he is satisfied with your design concepts, this language should reassure him.

The next question is, "What is your responsibility to complete the project for this figure?"

The first answer is, "An estimate is only an estimate." It is not a detailed budget that you have guaranteed. You will most likely not be bound to complete the project at that exact figure.

Once you have completed the initial presentation and indicated material selections, painting and wallcovering plans, and lighting fixtures, prepare a preliminary budget. This is an itemized list of general costs, not a series of specific estimates that will later be obtained from workmen and vendors—a final budget. A preliminary budget can be obtained through phone calls to vendors and workmen as you won't need detailed cost estimates.

If the preliminary budget falls within the $25,000 range (to continue using the previous example) and your client approves the initial presentation, make sure that he signs this budget before proceeding. Once this is done, you have satisfied the "projected estimate figure" in your letter of agreement and are taken off the hook. One assumes, of course, that the preliminary budget is reasonably accurate. The figures don't have to be precise, but prices should not fluctuate more than 5 percent of their projected cost.

If the preliminary budget goes way over, then another course of action is necessary. A meeting with your client is mandatory to explain why the cost is, for example, $7,500 more than the projected estimate. If the client wanted leather sofas, you could use a substitute fabric to reduce the estimate. A built-in wet bar may have to be eliminated. Those decisions are up to the client. You must be willing to redesign the space so that it will be satisfactory to the client at the projected estimate range. Just don't throw up your hands and refuse to try to reduce the cost. A projected estimate is still a commitment. If you show your client that you are willing to be flexible, he may back down and decide to spend more. Judgment and tact are crucial in handling this type of situation.

Let me describe an extreme example of how budgeting can be mishandled. One of my interior designer clients indicated in the letter of agreement that a client's one-bedroom apartment could be designed for $40,000—the projected estimate. The client signed the letter of agreement, and the project began. During the initial meeting, the client decided to add a number of custom items. The designer assumed that his client realized that costs would rise but said nothing. He was glad the budget was increasing because he was being paid on a percentage basis. Once the final budget was prepared, the cost was more than double the original figure. The designer tried to remedy the situation by taking out custom items. His client became irate, claimed the project should have been finished within the projected estimate range, and refused to listen to reason. The designer ended up losing the client and returning his design retainer, having spent days designing the space and conferring with workmen for no money.

The error on the part of the designer is obvious. When he realized that his client's needs would push the cost well in excess of the projected estimate, he should have advised the client immediately in person. He should have followed up this conversation with a letter indicating that the initial projected estimate did not include these items. If this had been resolved both orally and in writing early in the relationship, the outcome might have been different.

However, some designers who disregard this counsel have made a great deal of money, especially when working on cost-plus as opposed to a monthly or fixed fee. They tell their clients, for example, that they can design their living room for $25,000—their projected estimate in the letter of agreement. However, the client may decide that he wants a $10,000 Oriental rug or piece of antique furniture, leaving only $15,000 to finish the entire room. The designer purchases the item and warehouses it until final installation. Once the client sees the final budget, he is aware that the budget is now $35,000 because of that one costly purchase. The designer can say, "Well, we can always return the rug and be back on budget." But it is too late. The client knows he owns the rug and doesn't want to give it up. He decides to go ahead and finish the project despite the $10,000 increase. If the designer is working on a 25 percent commission, he has earned an additional $2,500 design fee by going over budget.

Many designers take these chances with their clients constantly. They quote a low budget to get the job, and once they are under contract, try to push the client into spending the absolute maximum. Unethical? Perhaps. You must understand the legal ramifications when using this strategy.

If a designer gives a client a projected estimate and then exceeds the figure dramatically, the client may properly contend that he is in breach of contract. Most clients, in my experience, will simply ask the designer to eliminate some of the more costly items if they decide not to spend the extra money. If they want the added luxuries badly enough, they will increase the budget. However, as I have mentioned, the designer runs the risk of being sued for his design fee, losing the client, and spending initial design time without compensation.

If a client requests a projected estimate in the letter of agreement and you are at all uncertain about what to state, play it conservatively. Base the projected estimate on your initial meetings during which you told him the truth about prices. Once the preliminary budget is finished, he must sign it before the final estimates are made. And, finally, if he does go over budget, be certain that all additions to the projected estimate are approved in writing.

I always advise designers to be extremely scrupulous about their responsibilities to clients; unfortunately, the reverse is not always true. Sometimes clients act irresponsibly, placing the designer in a very difficult situation financially with vendors as the following example illustrates:

I was once consulted by an interior designer in New York City who had been in business for over fifteen years. He was known in the trade as a society decorator. His clientele was small but select and used him on a repeat basis. He had a conflict involving his clients, a husband and wife, and a vendor, and upholsterer whom he used exclusively and whose quality and superb craftsmanship were vital to his career. Apparently, the wife went way over budget against her husband's wishes. The designer had no idea there was discord as he had previously worked only with the wife, on a former residence, and money never appeared to be a problem. In any event, after designing over $10,000 of custom upholstery, the designer instructed the upholsterer to start work and ordered the fabric to be charged to his own account. He then called the wife for a deposit. She told him (1) she could not afford it, (2) the order was never approved, and (3) he would have to reduce the cost of the upholstery. The designer complained that she had approved his drawings and fabric selections, and it was too late to cancel the orders. She replied that as far as she was concerned, it was his problem. She had signed no purchase orders, and as the designer charged retail, all goods were purchased on credit for his own account. The designer at first hoped that she and her husband would compromise, and she would decide to purchase the upholstery. But no luck. The upholsterer told him a month later that he was ready to deliver the furniture and wanted to be paid in full. When the designer stalled, he received a threatening letter from the upholsterer's lawyer, at which point he consulted me.

I advised the designer that several courses of action were available, but first he had to consider his responsibilities and priorities with all parties involved. Obviously, he couldn't satisfy everyone. Someone had to take a loss, and he had to decide who it would be before taking any action.

This particular upholsterer's quality and service had been crucial in establishing the designer's reputation. It is well known that fine craftsmen in the trade are not easy to find. Consequently, when a successful working relationship is established, it should be treated with great care and respect.

The designer had also to consider his own reputation. He had been in business for a number of years and was very well known in the design community. A designer's stock in trade includes his credit rating and reputation for integrity. Although many vendors refuse to accept orders from anyone without a 50 percent or more deposit, reputation still counts for public relations purposes and should be saved at any cost. Clients and potential clients will hear through the grapevine if a designer doesn't pay his bills. Publications and periodicals often overlook a designer with a double-dealing pedigree.

Certainly it is important to please clients, even those that don't always behave well. In this case, the designer had to be practical. The client was a repeat customer from a select social circle who would probably either use him again or recommend him to prosperous friends who would be eager to pay for his services.

The designer was left with the following alternatives. The vendor who sold the fabric had to be paid or the designer's credit would have been ruined. The upholsterer had to be paid or the designer would have lost a key workman. And, finally, the client had to be accommodated if the designer was to finish the job and obtain others. Resolution of all these elements required my client to a swallow his pride and open his wallet.

If you find yourself in an analogous situation between your client and vendors, contemplate using this strategy. Begin by sending checks for small amounts to the vendor(s), the fabric house, and the upholsterer to demonstrate your good faith. As the designer owed the fabric house $3,000, he sent 10 percent immediately—before delinquent bills began arriving. Simultaneously with issuing payment, call the vendor and explain the situation. Try to stall for time. My client owed his upholsterer $10,000: He sent $1,000 with a bottle of champagne and asked him to hold the merchandise and requests for further payment for 30 days. If you can bargain for that amount of breathing space, by the time the period has elapsed, you'll know where you stand. Because the orders for merchandise were taken from the designer without client approval, he was legally responsible for final payment in any event. Therefore, he wasn't waiving any of his legal rights by making small payments.

Now comes the hardest part. Contact your client at once. Review the situation and apologize for the misunderstanding even though you know you were not at fault. Be a sport and offer to waive your commission or design fee on one particular item. In this case, it was upholstery. If that doesn't work, find out what your client would be willing to spend. If the client offers 70 percent or better of your net cost, settle it, pay the rest out of your pocket, and forget it.

Now, everyone will be happy. You will have saved face and acted as a gentleman. A loss of several thousand dollars was not overwhelming for the designer in the example. Of course, you'll have to weigh the loss in terms of your own business and arrive at your own conclusion. If you retain an attorney and drag the matter into litigation, you'll spend that amount or even more on fees and will lose a source and a client.

The designer in the case absorbed a $2,500 loss. However, he earned a total design fee exceeding $15,000 and received two other referrals from this client within six months. If, however, your client refuses to accept the merchandise on generous terms, you may then have to resort to legal means. An arbitration clause in your letter of agreement makes it possible to resolve the matter in one series of hearings without appeal. As has been discussed, this will reduce time, effort, and legal bills. Assure your vendors that they will receive indemnification for the cost of the goods. If you are legally responsible for payment and will require their cooperation ultimately, this only makes sense. Finally, one additional cost must be absorbed that cannot be measured in dollars and sense—the aggravation cost.

Once you extricate yourself from a predicament of this

nature, the following axioms should be branded in your memory forever. When charging retail, always have your clients sign detailed purchase orders issued by your firm before you place orders with vendors. If you can obtain full payment in advance, (pro forma), do so. This applies to design commissions as well, which should be added to net cost to become a retail figure. These orders should thoroughly describe the items on order, and if the goods are custom, a sketch with dimensions should be attached. Also, remember that a husband and wife must both be involved, at least to the extent that they jointly sign all orders. Operating in any other way is not only unprofessional but an invitation to disaster.

In the previous example, my client had to compromise to maintain relations with his vendors and to please the client as well. Most designers wouldn't argue against that behavior at such a relatively small cost.

Under certain circumstances, you may be duped by a client, and consequently, may not want to maintain any further relationship with him. Still, your responsibilities to certain vendors may make it provident to settle for less than your due. The following is a typical situation in which compromise was necessary:

A young interior designer in metropolitan Chicago had been retained the previous year by a wealthy builder to design a model apartment for a thirty-story luxury building. The designer had also rented an apartment for his own use in the building. The builder had been paying for all the goods and construction as the job progressed. The budget was approximately $100,000 and the designer

had earned $28,000 in fees and commissions at the time
trouble developed. When the builder was sent a final
set of bills for $2,700 in design commissions and
$9,000 for accessories manufactured by a specialty firm
in New York, he refused to pay but gave no explanation.
He simply told the designer that he had paid enough and
that was that. The manufacturer sued the designer for
non-payment, but the designer's lawyer brought the builder into the lawsuit. When the designer contacted me, the
builder still refused to pay for any design commissions
but offered to settle for $9,000, the cost of the merchan-
dise. The designer had already paid his attorney a $1,200
fee and was advised to settle by his counsel. He was
very angry and didn't want to swallow the loss.

I told the designer that his attorney's advice was correct.
Further, I advised him to settle the claim immediately
before the offer was withdrawn and to consider himself
fortunate for concluding a potentially hazardous episode
so economically.

The problem had arisen through the designer's sloppy
business practices. Specialty accessories generally require
either a 50 percent deposit on order with the balance plus
design commissions due prior to delivery or pro forma payment upon issuance of the order. Obviously, delivery was
made in this situation before outstanding balances were
paid.

As the example indicated, payment did not stop until the
job was nearly completed. Clients, unlike leopards, often
change their spots for no apparent reason when it comes
to paying bills. Do not be lulled into a sense of security by a

client's stable credit record. Simply tell a client that certain deposits must be made regardless of your past relationship. Explain that this is nothing personal and that no negative inferences are intended. It is simply a question of uniform business practice for all of your clientele. The wealthy builder in the example would have understood that language very well; consequently, if he had been unhappy with the designer's work at any point, he would have expressed his feelings before any losses had been sustained.

Because there was no indication that the builder was in financial difficulty, we must assume that he chose simply not to pay his bills. If you find yourself locked into such a grudge match, settle it quickly. A client may be dissatisfied with a designer's work or feel that he has been overcharged. His motivation is not important. You have to minimize your losses as much as you can.

Young interior designers generally have neither the funds nor the energy to waste in minor litigation. Consider also that in a lawsuit, the client—the defendant being sued for the cost of merchandise and fees—has the option to make a counterclaim against a designer—the plaintiff—in an amount exceeding the designer's and the manufacturer's claim. True, this counterclaim may be groundless and without merit. But, nonetheless, a counterclaim by a persistent counsel can result in soaring legal bills. Wealthy commercial clients usually have formidable weapons that they will often use without hesitation or even good reason.

Designers cannot generally afford to absorb too many losses in the early stages of their career. Accordingly, as I have explained, they are almost compelled to use an arbitration clause in the letter of agreement to avoid the type of lawsuit that was instituted against the designer in the example.

Parenthetically, the fact that the designer was a tenant in his client's building had no effect on the legal action. Neither party was entitled to relate their landlord-tenant relationship to that matter. For example, if the designer had withheld rent to offset his commissions, he could have been evicted summarily.

The designer's indignation at having to absorb this loss was certainly understandable. The job had been completed, and his compensation was not only arbitrarily denied but his credibility with a vendor had been destroyed.

If the designer had contacted me before the vendor sued him, I would have given him the following advice: Because the vendor is an important one, go to any length to satisfy him. The designer should have guaranteed the vendor payment regardless of the outcome of the lawsuit. He should never have charged the merchandise to his own account or released it to his client prior to full payment. However, once he did both these things he should have assumed responsibility for payment.

Unfortunately, a few clients will always try to squeeze a designer at the end of a project. Guard yourself against this by signed purchase orders, deposits, and arbitration clauses. However, when you fail to do this and suffer the consequences, don't compound your error. Retrench, consolidate, and learn from your mistakes.

In all three examples about balancing responsibilities

with clients and vendors, there is one common thread. Either the designer was concerned about making a mistake (in the first example) or has already made one (the second and third examples). No interior design firm can run a mistake-proof business. So many things can go wrong, and, sooner or later, something does. Take as many precautions as you can. Remember if something in an important relationship fails, consider your priorities before making a decision and taking action.

Reacting When a Client Changes His Mind

Unfortunately for designers and vendors, clients often change their minds about completed design plans or ordered merchandise even after they have approved them. Substitutions or changes can be handled more easily if the order is not custom, if the change is made prior to shipment, or if work has not yet begun. Very often, however, clients request changes or demand substitutions after their orders or plans have gone past the point of no return. Designers and vendors are then in uncomfortable, if not costly, positions.

Here is a typical "last minute change" in which the vendor, who tried to be cooperative, was wedged between the designer and his client and had no idea as to how to react. I have related the dilemma from the vendor's point of view to show the designer how a custom supplier thinks when the ultimate consumer, the client, tries to victimize them both:

I was consulted by the owner of a small furniture and accessories manufacturing company that produced all merchandise on a custom basis as ordered through designers. Two months prior to the consultation, a designer had ordered a $2,500 cocktail table for his client. He had specified a 36-inch round table lacquered in Chinese red with an octagonal brushed-brass base. A 50 percent deposit accompanied the order, which was standard procedure with his firm. About two weeks later, before work began, the designer called the owner and said the client wanted the lacquer color changed to beige, the shape of the base to round, and the base finish to stainless steel. The owner made the changes on the purchase order but did not issue a new one and called his craftsmen to make the changes. When the table arrived seven weeks later and was ready for delivery, the designer and client came to inspect it. When the client saw the table, she was horrified. She told the owner and the designer that she wanted the table as originally ordered, that she had only mentioned possible changes in the color and base, and that she had never meant these changes to be more than suggestions. The designer protested and said that she had insisted on the changes and had to pay for the order. The client steadfastly refused to accept delivery unless her table conformed to the original specifications and blamed the designer for the error. The designer had been an old and trusted customer, and the owner wanted advice on the fairest way to proceed as well as clarification about his own legal responsibilities.

I advised the owner that, of course, he was probably not legally liable. His merchandise was sold only through designers, so he was responsible to the designer, not the client. This is usually the case unless a purchase order specifically indicates that an owner may deal directly with the client without the designer's immediate supervision. The rationale for this relationship is very simple. The owner's merchandise was sold to a wholesale market. His customers, i.e., designers, made profits on the resale of the merchandise by obtaining the consumers (clients) and specifying the nature of the goods to be manufactured. Designers had to keep their clients under control and insure that there were no errors in processing orders as a result of the changes.

In this example the owner had handled the order in the proper manner. The initial purchase order prescribed definite requirements with an adequate description of the merchandise to be manufactured. Before work started, the owner's customer, the designer, issued specific changes and written notes were made to confirm the changes in plans. Ideally, the owner should have issued a new purchase order to the designer and had him initial his approval. Alternatively, it would have been smart to have correspondence confirming the telephone conversation in which the changes in question were requested. However, as matters stood, the owner was still in a fairly secure position.

The designer could have claimed that the changes were never officially requested but merely discussed and insisted that the owner was responsible for compliance with the terms of the initial purchase order. The designer, however, was honest and admitted in front of the client and the owner's employees that he had specifically requested changes.

If the designer had not been candid and *had* claimed that the changes were never requested, it would have been the owner's word against the designer's in a legal proceeding.

How could the owner have substantiated his own position? In most states, books and records kept in the ordinary course of business are accepted as credible evidence. The burden of proof is then shifted to the designer who must prove that those records are false or incorrect. He could, of course, prepare his own correspondence or alter records indicating the confirmation of the initial order. Of course, any court or jury would seriously question the veracity of this documentation.

In its final determination, a court, after proof is submitted by both parties, decides what in fact makes sense. It certainly seems unlikely that the owner would have made such drastic changes unless they had been specifically requested, especially as those changes were routinely recorded on the owner's records.

The owner in the case did not, in fact, go to court. The designer was a good customer, so the owner wanted to do everything possible to insure continued patronage.

Often clients change their minds yet again when faced with reality. Consequently, the owner tried to resolve the situation with the least amount of conflict. First of all, he offered to deliver the controversial table to the client's residence. Improbable as it seems, this tactic is often successful. When an item is seen in place in the room, the client often begins to like it and wants to keep it.

The owner then gave the designer an alternative if that strategy should fail. He offered to relacquer the table and revise the base at his own cost if the designer would absorb the difference. This was very expensive, so he offered to sell the table to the designer at cost, i.e., below wholesale price. He suggested placing the table on his showroom floor with a substantially reduced price that did not include a manufacturer's or designer's mark-up. The owner believed the table would sell quickly at the low price, thus saving both the owner and designer a lot of money. Until the sale was made, the risk of loss was to be borne by the designer. The owner would merely act as an agent, i.e., would handle the transaction on a consignment basis.

During the time the table would be for sale, the owner offered to accommodate the designer further by manufacturing its replacement at his own cost. The designer's mark-up would then substantially reimburse him for the loss on the first table if it didn't sell or had to be reduced further. Of course, once the sale was made, the owner then wanted to take his mark-up.

By providing all these options, the owner certainly felt that he had done his part. In any custom business, incidents of this nature invariably occur. Loss of profits in such cases must be accepted as part of the cost of doing business.

The designer's client finally accepted the table with the existing base and a relacquered top, which the designer paid for at the owner's cost. The designer was fortunate to end the episode so cheaply and naturally continued doing business with the owner. The designer had learned the hard way how he could be victimized by a client.

The "change of mind" in the previous example is typical of many cases. Clients are frequently overwhelmed by anxiety after a purchase is made even with their decorator's assistance, and they feel that they must make some change. In some cases, clients change their minds about proceeding with the whole project after all plans have been approved, as the following cases will illustrate:

> I was consulted by a New York designer specializing in the architectural renovation of residential interiors. A year ago, he had been retained by a client who wanted his townhouse totally redesigned. He was paid a $5,000 flat design fee plus 30 percent commission on all purchases of goods and construction. The visual presentation was approved. All construction drawings were prepared. About a week before the plans were sent out for bids, the client put the house on the market and sold it two months later. Shortly thereafter, he bought a large apartment in a high-rise building overlooking the city. He then contacted the designer to design his new apartment. The designer offered him the same terms as specified by their prior agreement—a $5,000 design fee plus 30 percent commission on all purchases. The designer explained that the previous project did not relate in any way to the new apartment and that all the former plans and presentations had no value. The designer asked me if he had to give the client any credit for his work.

I informed the designer that he was completely in the clear and was not required to give any credit in regard to his design of the townhouse.

Fortunately, the services now to be rendered for the design fee were documented in writing. Let me emphasize the importance of precision in your letter of agreement. As indicated in Chapter One, the first paragraph of the agreement should always contain a clause locating and describing the space to be designed and the areas of this space for an initial design fee of $5,000. If he were to be listed.

In this case, the designer had agreed to design the entire space for an initial design fee for $5,000. If he were to design only part of the house, he could have faced problems even before the project was called off. For instance, suppose this fee covered the designer's costs for only five of the rooms. At some later date, the client could have requested additional plans and insisted on their preparation at no cost to him. The client could also have conceivably changed his mind about *which* rooms he wanted designed. The designer would have been forced to comply with the client's request because of the failure of his agreement to spell out his specific obligations.

Designers must obtain reasonable deposits even if they are working on commissions for purchases of goods and construction. Generally, a designer spends a great amount of time on initial consultations and preliminary plans and construction drawings. Design fees, no matter whether they are flat amounts or retainers to be applied against commissions, partially cover the cost of initial efforts but generally do not cover services rendered to that juncture. The real profits come later when purchases are made and the commissions are collected. In the example, the initial design fee did not fully remunerate the designer for his time. All drawings had been completed.

Many design contracts provide that as soon as all purchase orders are completed and approved in writing by the client, the commissions are due even if the client changes his mind and decides not to proceed. However, this is a tough clause to negotiate, and very often designers are loathe to use it for fear of losing the job. Potential clients usually insist that it implies a gross mistrust and, especially in the early stages of the relationship, do not want to be committed to spending specific amounts of money before they even see any plans.

How should the designer handle such a client? If the client we have been talking about refused to pay the new fee, the relationship would have ended. Had he threatened a lawsuit, the likelihood of a court determining that the designer had any liability was very slim. Because this client finally relented and agreed to pay a new design fee, I simply told the designer to consider carefully whether to continue handling the project at all. First, he had lost money on the initial episode and had difficulty with the client. Second, if the client changed his mind once, he certainly could do so again.

A design project that is completed and never executed is very frustrating for a designer. You lose not only financially but emotionally. You also lose a potential subject for your portfolio and for publication. This point is not as crucial for a large concern with a substantial number of projects in progress, but a small, growing organization needs examples to show prospective clients.

Before deciding whether to turn the client away, my client considered his responsibilities. He and his client had gradually developed an extended personal relationship. The client's taste, needs, and budget were explored, and solutions were found. Obviously, the client had enough respect for the designer's abilities to seek his services again.

When the designer decided to risk a second relationship, I told him to be especially careful with the budget. Many designers do not prepare a budget with the initial visual presentation because if the client disapproves, it all has to be substantially redone with a double amount of time expended. You may get away with omitting the budget if you and the client are on the same wave length at the start of the project.

The designer naturally proceeded with caution here. He prepared a fairly detailed budget with his visual presentation and had the client initial all the selections he approved. When changes were made, these were approved in the same manner. The designer left very little room for error before having any of the construction drawings prepared. The client approved the drawings in writing as well before submitting them for bids. The job subsequently was completed fairly quickly, and the designer was fully paid.

Another situation in which clients will change their minds about a design project, regardless of its stage of completion, happens to most interior designers at least once in their career, as the following illustrates:

A residential designer in the Houston area had been retained by a married couple to redesign and complete all installations for their large suburban home. The budget, minus the design fee, was in excess of $200,000. When the project was about half finished after six months, the couple argued and the husband moved out. The wife then advised the designer that she couldn't pay his commissions or the bills for the furnishings that were to be delivered in approximately one month. The designer was at a loss.

Dealing with a couple who become estranged in the middle of a design project requires finesse, perserverance, and determination. In this situation, it didn't sound as if the designer could realistically expect to complete the job. He had to extricate himself as quickly as possible, collect his fees for services performed, and secure payment for those vendors with goods on order or contractors with work in progress.

The exact steps which you must take under similar circumstances will depend upon your method of operation as outlined by your letter of agreement. But the husband and wife must sign the contract to insure joint responsibility. Some designers operate on a "direct payment" method, under which their clients pay vendors and contractors directly and the designers supply supervision and purchase orders. Consequently, the designer is literally liability-free except for the collection of his own fee. However, if the designer has purchased goods and services for the client either retail or cost plus, and the accounts with vendors are in the designer's name, a variety of alternatives should be considered.

First, the designer should immediately contact the husband and request comprehensive accounting. In the example, the husband was affluent and realized that he was responsible for payment. If a husband is not irrational, usually a solution can be found. The designer should be entirely candid and tell the husband that he probably will not choose to continue with the project regardless of what the couple decides to do. Even if a couple does ultimately reconcile and decides to complete the job, it is probably unwise for the designer to resume. Once a designer is warned that a client may fail to meet his obligations, it is best to end the relationship. If the responsible party refuses either to cooperate or confer with the designer, document all claims and mail the accounting by certified or registered mail to both husband and wife.

As previously indicated, notify all vendors and contractors by telephone immediately and confirm by written memorandum.

If the designer's letter of agreement has been properly structured, problems should be minimized. For example, full payment and design commissions should be requested on order for wallpaper, fabrics, lighting fixtures, accessories, plants and retail items, i.e., flatware, china, crystal, linen, and other household items. Although the designer may not actually pay all these vendors in full before delivery, the client's money should be on deposit.

For other furnishings and fixtures, 50 percent of wholesale cost and design fees should be deposited with the designer on order. Cancellation fees rarely run this high, so this deposit will protect the designer. Certain vendors will cancel orders on stock items for a minimal charge. As I have mentioned, custom-ordered merchandise may present different problems, and manufacturers have varying policies. If work is not yet in progress on the order, cancellation should be simple. If the items are ready for shipment, often a manufacturer will cancel the order when a substantial deposit is forfeited. When the manufacturer insists on full payment and delivery and the order is placed in the designer's name solely, the designer has a problem. In rare situations, the designer may be forced to accept the merchandise and seek legal recourse from his client.

Antiques do not generally present too much of a problem. If the designer has a good working relationship with reputable dealers, they will often accept the merchandise and give a full refund.

On labor and construction, a 50 percent deposit on wholesale cost and design fees should be paid to the designer upon purchase order approval by the client. In this connection, many contractors refuse to proceed with custom installations unless they are paid at each stage of their work. Therefore, if the parties refuse to continue payment, monies for most of the work performed to date should have been held on deposit.

Let's now consider the grimmest of all possibilities. If the designer did not obtain sufficient deposits from his clients and has ordered a considerable amount of custom-made merchandise for his own account, he may require legal help. If you ever are in this situation, don't wait. Institution of proceedings may frighten either or both parties into immediate restitution. Advise all unpaid vendors about the situation, and they may join you in the action. If an arbitration clause was present in the letter of agreement, relief may be speedy and inexpensive. Just remember that if payment is due and appears not to be forthcoming, a designer should not stall vendors and destroy his own credit rating, one of his most valuable assets. Make the vendors aware of the situation and take immediate corrective measures.

When billing on a cost-plus basis, I always stipulate that payment for design fee commissions is due on all goods and services for which purchase orders are prepared and approved in writing by the client. Therefore, even if the client cancels the order, the fee is still payable to the designer. If the client denies liability for these commissions but will pay cancellation fees for the goods he no longer wants, the designer must decide whether he should bother to use legal means to collect his fee.

Generally, when a designer is faced with such a situation, his initial reaction is one of shock and bewilderment. However, quite frequently, resolution of the financial difficulties is quick if the designer takes immediate corrective measures to compel his clients to recognize their responsibilities and meet their obligations.

When the designer pressed the accounting on the Houston husband in the example, the husband paid immediately, and the designer was bailed out. Under similar circumstances, you might not be that lucky on the first round, so remember *all* of this strategy.

In this chapter I have presented three examples of how clients frequently change their mind. One very important point should be grasped here. In each example, if the designer had been managing his business properly, any losses should have been the client's problem not the designer's. Isn't that logical! Thus, as the designer, you must take responsibility to avoid misplaced liabilities caused by the whims or mistakes of clients.

Handling Trouble on the Job

Up to this point the problems discussed have not, for the most part, been insurmountable. As the examples illustrate, the difficulties either could have been eliminated or at least greatly minimized by the proper letter of agreement and good organization of ongoing projects. However, at times, as illustrated by the following example, a designer must be prepared to cope with real trouble:

An interior designer who had designed and supervised the construction of a suite of commercial offices called me six months after the project had been completed. His client had just contacted him in a very angry frame of mind. Some of the installations were falling apart, and he blamed the designer. The wallcoverings were buckling, the carpentry and paint looked shoddy and were defective, and some of the custom cabinet work had begun to delaminate. (The client had insisted on a contractor who had done a lot of work in his office building, despite other suggestions and recommendations by the designer.) The client claimed the problems were the result of inappropriate materials and improper supervision. The client was irate, and the designer needed advice as to how to respond.

I advised the designer not to panic. As he insisted that he had performed his services with the amount of diligence and professional competence required, I did not feel that he had any liability for his client's damages.

Because the client selected the building contractor and

dealt with him directly, the designer could not be held liable for defective workmanship. He had not been a party to the relationship, and, on the contrary, had recommended other workmen.

Under similar circumstances when supervising construction for a client, your obligations are: (1) provision of a workable design plan and specification of appropriate materials and (2) supervision of workmanship.

The defects in the example did not arise from errors made on construction drawings, schedules, sketches, or floor plans. For instance, there was no improper partitioning of an area as could have resulted from errors on a partition drawing or plan. Further, the designer had prepared purchase orders for all goods and services specified, a standard procedure. These purchase orders served as a record of the designer's competence in terms of material authorization and had been signed by the client prior to submission to the vendors and contractors.

A specific problem was the buckling of wall coverings. Obviously, that damage can stem from a number of different sources unrelated to the designer's work. The use of the wrong adhesive, improper application, or leaks in the walls of the structure itself can all cause buckling. The responsibility of the designer is to select the appropriate materials for the surfaces being covered and to specify the manner of application as recommended by the manufacturer.

The designer had specified the appropriate wall coverings and a particular adhesive for application. The selection had been documented with a purchase order approved by the client. Further, he had supervised the installation, noting that the contractor had adhered to his paint and wallcovering schedule and the manufacturer's instructions for application. As no material deviations had been made, it wasn't necessary for the designer to contact his client. But if you are supervising applications of this nature and so become aware that the contractor is ignoring the manufacturer's specifications and your advice, tell you client immediately and send him a written memorandum to protect yourself from any subsequent reprisals.

In fact, some designers refuse to undertake projects unless they feel that the contractor has the technical competence to implement their design plans. Most designers, unfortunately, don't have that luxury as the example illustrates. Accordingly, if a contractor refuses to acknowledge your supervision, you can only document every error or deviation during the course of the job and be certain that the client receives written memoranda to this effect.

You are not totally responsible for the specification of materials and supervision of workmanship. Even if you make an error or omission, the contractor shares the responsibility. Not only is the work to be performed according to minimum standards of craftsmanship, specifications are to be checked as well. For this reason as well as others, it is most advantageous to the client if the designer and contractor have had previous successful work experiences and developed a good rapport.

In the example, the designer advised his client that the material specification was appropriate and that he had adequately supervised the installation. He also mentioned that any damage was the result of the contractor's inadequate performance and reminded the client that he had recommended another contractor.

The client, unfortunately, wasn't pacified with this explanation and replied, that surely, the designer must have seen the poor quality of workmanship during the project. The designer then showed copies of three letters that he had sent his client during the project. Each letter was a criticism of the supervision and quality of the work by the general contractor. The client said that he had never received these letters.

Ultimately the case went to court, and the designer was sued as a co-defendant with the contractor. The designer presented his own evidence on "summary judgment" and was dismissed as a co-defendant before the case ever went to trial.

In any event, if you ever become enmeshed in a similar situation, respond to your client at once. Indicate that you would be willing to help supervise the repairs but also advise that you have satisfied your obligations and are only acting now out of goodwill. Don't be placed in a defensive position when you are not responsible for any damages!

The previous example was a situation in which the designer was completely blameless. He had handled the project properly and, when a lawsuit resulted, was not held liable for any damages.

In the following example, trouble resulted from the designer's unprofessional approach to design and supervision:

An interior designer from Los Angeles, best known for his contemporary interiors with custom installations, consulted me when faced with a crisis. He had designed a mirrored sliding door for a client who had been thrilled with the concept. He had had the door built by an expert carpenter. It was hung on a track that was bolted into the ceiling. After construction was completed, the mirror work was applied at considerable expense by one of the finest mirror vendors in Southern California. No bottom track had been installed but neither the designer, carpenter, or the mirror vendors thought it necessary. Apparently, it was. One panel shattered on the top because the door swung too freely. At this point, a track was installed. The designer called the carpenter and the mirror vendors to help determine the exact cause of the damage. All were very quick to disclaim liability and refuse to assume any part of the loss. In fact, the designer believed that the panel may have cracked from other causes, but the client insisted that disaster struck because there was no track. Of course, the client assumed that the designer would either pay for the damage or cause the appropriate vendors to repair the door without charge. Although the designer had not yet said so to the client, he told me that he didn't feel in any way responsible. He claimed that he had been retained by his client because of his unique design ability, that all other aspects of the job were innovative and had been completed perfectly. As far as he was concerned, the damage was a "design casualty" to be accepted by his client. However, he was still worried about being obligated to make restitution and considered suing the carpenter and mirror supplier.

This was a typical situation wherein the problem required an analysis of professional responsibilities prior to instituting a course of action. Unfortunately, some of the most innovative and creative designers miss the obvious and fail to utilize common sense when resolving trouble on the job.

This designer emphasized that he had achieved his reputation with custom designs requiring special installations. Whatever else a design may be it must first be capable of being constructed and reasonably fit for its purpose. The responsibility for these two requirements rests overwhelmingly upon the designer.

The designer's approach disturbed me for two reasons. First, he had defended himself by saying that all other aspects of the job had been completed with no problem. Why shouldn't they have been? That fact deserves no special gold star and certainly can't be utilized to justify errors.

Second, the designer mentioned that he had been retained because of his unique design ability and emphasized that a client should accept a casualty or so per job without question because of the special value of his creative services. That attitude is not only offensive but totally unprofessional.

A designer with a different outlook might have taken the same or even greater risks and simultaneously minimized his own liability by the following procedures. In this situation, for example, the designer conceived the design, believed execution to be a realistic possibility, and then "sold" it to the client. He had been careful enough to select the finest craftsmen to execute the concept. However, it was his first experience with creating that particular kind of device, which was constructed of very fragile and expensive material and had to be functional as well as decorative.

If you are ever in the same situation, consult with the craftsmen subsequent to design completion. If they have reservations, note them and proceed with caution. Then, talk to the client. Tell him the truth: The design is new; it should work, but the material is fragile. Do not guarantee total success and indicate that a specific percentage of the initial construction cost should be added into the estimate, over and above the original figure, as a margin for error in the event of changes. Explain that this is a common procedure when creating a prototype.

It is simply amazing, despite all these warnings, that clients will proceed nonetheless. In any event, the designer can protect himself even if the outcome is less than ideal. If no damage results, the designer becomes a hero; if a casualty does occur at least the client had been forewarned. Take these precautions in advance and in writing. Further, if the client does change his mind and decides not to bear the financial risk, the designer will have saved himself from a headache. Some other client will take the chance at a later date.

Obviously, it was too late for the designer in the example to use these tactics. He had to repair the damage immediately to rectify his relationship with his client. As the client had not been forewarned about potential damage, he had naturally expected his designer to assume full responsibility.

As far as litigation with his craftsmen was concerned, I

advised the designer to ask himself several questions that should be contemplated by all designers before suing a vendor. Are their services unique? Will you have to use them again? Were you cautioned by them before any damage occured? If so, were you warned in writing? Was the installation itself properly completed, i.e., the track hung securely, the mirror work finished properly, etc.? It is obvious that if a designer's instructions are followed and if he has no objections upon completion of work, it is unlikely that he will have any recourse whatsoever against the craftsmen.

The fact that a subsequent installation of a track corrected the problem was a further indictment of the designer's guilt. He found the solution but too late. Even if the damage had arisen from causes other than the absence of the track, the designer couldn't prove it or convince the client that such was the case.

Ultimately, the designer ended up paying for everything—a very costly outcome. Always remember one crucial point before embarking on this kind of venture. An innovative designer who wants his client to take risks to satisfy mutual creative endeavors must develop great skill and style in client relations. Otherwise, he should only specify the safest and most predictable design solutions and installations that will meet his client's needs.

Thus far, the problems we have been discussing have resulted, basically, from poor workmanship, inferior material quality, and design error. Sometimes, however, a designer may find himself entangled in the personal affairs of his client in such a way as to cause the worst kind of trouble. If he has not run his financial affairs with a certain degree of precision, he may find himself in the most adverse circumstances as the following example illustrates:

I had been consulted by a very successful New York designer who had always operated on an informal basis with his wealthy and prominent clientele. However, he unexpectedly ran into some real trouble and didn't know how to handle it. Two of his old clients were a very rich and powerful real estate executive and his wife with whom he had a cordial relationship of long standing. Six months prior to the time he conferred with me, these clients had contacted him to completely redesign their twelve-room duplex. He did so, the budget being well in excess of $500,000. The clients approved the design and presentation and told the designer to proceed and process all orders. Actual construction was completed and paid for; all furniture, fabrics, and accessories were ordered. The designer never made these clients approve any purchase orders in writing, but they had supplied him with 50 percent deposits where specified by the vendors. The remainder of the orders had been charged to the designer's open accounts at vendors where he had established credit. Toward the end of the job, the husband and wife separated, the husband intending to remarry as soon as his divorce was final. The designer had several meetings with the husband and his fiancee. She wanted everything changed and told the designer that she didn't particularly care for his work. Up until that point, the designer had handled all bookkeeping and payment, without any difficulty, with the husband's office administrative assistant. Since the balances outstanding exceeded $150,000 for merchandise yet to be delivered, the designer was in a state of total panic. He feared, of course, that he would never be paid for the merchandise because the fiancee didn't like it and he would have to reimburse the vendors himself.

This predicament was one of the worst in which I had ever known a residential designer to become entrapped. In a simple divorce situation, such as the example mentioned in the previous chapter, a designer can usually extricate himself without too much trouble. Here, however, the designer had unwittingly become involved in a situation that placed him in great financial jeopardy.

A designer's informal style of conducting business can prove to be a very expensive mistake. Too often, a designer is awed by his clientele, and if the relationship also develops into a social one, he loses perspective on *the* most important fact: He is running a business.

This situation is a typical illustration of how, even under the most favorable conditions, an unexpected event can cause insurmountable problems. Nothing should have gone wrong. First, the designer had been in business for a considerable length of time, was experienced and had rich clients. Second, he had worked well with the clients before, or his services would not have been retained again. Unlucky? Definitely. But sooner or later, such complications will crop up, and if you haven't organized a tight and sound operation, you will wind up losing money.

One thing, I advised the designer, was certain. He was finished with this client forever. The husband's new wife would be determined to dispose of everything the first wife had liked, which, of course, included the designer.

Although the designer had prepared purchase orders for

goods on order, neither the husband nor the wife had signed them. This was most unfortunate. A client's written acknowledgement of an order substantially removes financial liability from a designer, assuming there is compliance with the specifications. Improper ordering procedure was the designer's first mistake.

His second mistake was charging all purchases for the client to his own account. Never assume any financial responsibility for third parties if it can be avoided. Use your own credit line for your own purchases. In this situation, instead of obtaining the proper deposits, the designer paid for everything himself. Not only should the client have advanced these monies to the vendors, but he should also have paid design commissions on the deposits as the designer charged on a cost-plus basis. When the designer consulted me, payment had not yet been refused on ordered merchandise. However, he knew that trouble was on the horizon and was more than apprehensive.

The designer ultimately found the perfect easy way out. He prepared all purchase orders from scratch on all goods on order that had not been delivered and accepted. He included all deposits that he had charged to his own accounts and requested immediate payment for those. As he had always dealt with the client's office administrative assistant, he continued to submit all the documents to him. He inserted a note with the purchase orders requesting the client's signature, and when the office administrator questioned him, he advised that he was now processing orders this way. He didn't appear anxious, and the orders were finally signed. Fortunately, this was all done at the client's office away from the scrutiny of the client's new wife. Once the papers were signed, they ratified the orders legally by "relating back" as if they had originally been placed in that fashion.

I warned the designer that it was possible that the entire matter might be forced to a head prematurely. For example, when faced with the purchase orders, the client might have just told the designer that he wanted the project stopped and would make no further payment for goods on order. If the client had intended to refuse payment, he wouldn't have paid upon delivery in any event. Thus, the change of tactics really could not adversely affect the outcome.

If payment had been refused, the designer would have been forced to go to court. I generally advise every other avenue of recourse before advocating legal action. However, if payment had not been forthcoming quickly, drastic steps would have been necessary. When he wants to discard his designer, the client often resists dealing with him on any level as he realizes that any future relationship is out of the question. In situations of this nature, a lawsuit forces settlement because the designer is already a very painful burden for the client and a heavy-handed legal action may conclude dealings quickly and favorably. The designer becomes a thorn that must be removed.

The past three examples and, I'm certain, your own experience, have shown you that handling trouble on the job is one of the most draining and nonproductive aspects of an interior design business. The most frustrating aspect of all is that you cannot always protect yourself. Of course, if your business has been managed properly, the ramifications should be less severe. Remember that you must deal with trouble immediately. It's the only effective recourse.

CHAPTER FOUR:

Preparing a Letter of Agreement for Commercial Projects

Chapter One has already provided a general analysis of the letter of agreement. That discussion is relevant and pertinent to nearly any interior design contract regardless of the size or type of project.

Design contracts for corporate clients use a special language. Most languages have many dialects. Obviously, all variations of corporate contracts (their dialects) cannot be presented here. This chapter will show you how to prepare a letter of agreement for corporate clients with an architectural format. Frequent references will be made to the material in Chapter One.

The Area to be Designed

The style of corporate contracts is succinct but thorough, as the following example illustrates:

Mr. Eugene Smith
Secretary and Director
Real Estate Facilities
Corporate Real Estate Department
The XYZ Corporation

8000 Fifth Avenue
New York, New York

Dear Mr. Smith:

The following is our letter of agreement describing our interior design services for the following project:

The Acme Building
5555 Park Avenue
New York, New York 10000
Executive and Finance Group (approximately 300 persons)
Floors 8, 9, and 10
20,000 Square Feet per Floor
Total: 60,000 Square Feet
Occupancy Date: January 1, 1982

Note the specificity of the title of the corporate officer in charge of the project. This is to make sure that you are dealing with the properly authorized party. The number of persons who are to occupy the space is given to let the client know from the beginning that the designers recognize needs and requirements.

Services Provided-Introduction

After the opening paragraph, corporate contracts frequently preface the description of services to be provided as follows:

The services that we will provide will be outlined as follows. It is our understanding that the construction for all three floors will be building standard and that the furniture and furnishings will be new. You have advised us that XYZ has prepared standards for furniture and furnishings that will serve as the guide for outfitting the spaces. The building owner will provide both mechanical and electrical engineering services and architectural and contract documents.

Corporate designers usually present a client with all the given facts in this area. In the example "building standard" construction is delineated, a crucial factor when preparing construction drawings. Any services to be provided by the client—e.g., mechanical and electrical engineering services—should be mentioned even if there has been an oral understanding to that effect. Both services are so costly that the designer should state in writing that he will have no responsibility for their provision.

Services Provided-Phase Development

One of the major differences between architecturally oriented corporate contracts and general interior design contracts is that the description of services is organized into phases. The following is a typical example of phase development:

(Design Corporation) will provide the following required services in four (4) phases:
1. Programming / Building Analysis
2. Schematics / Design Development
3. Contract Documents and Fixtures and Furnishings Contract Documents
4. Construction Coordination

(Design Corporation's) work will be organized into these four phases, which will be undertaken in sequence. All phases of these services will include the following project management.

Project Management

Prior to the detailed description of the work undertaken in each phase, project management as provided by the designer is briefly outlined. The most common types of project management described at this stage of the agreement are Budget Control and Schedule Maintenance as the following example illustrates:

Budget Control. Early in the project (Design Corporation) will prepare a comprehensive cost estimate of the project work for XYZ's review and approval. This preliminary figure will serve to establish a target for cost control of the project. As the project progresses, (Design Corporation) will continually update estimates and submit them for XYZ's review and approval. Project Budgets will be submitted at the end of each phase.

Schedule Maintenance. All schedules in chart form and reports necessary for the orderly administration of this project shall be prepared by (Design Corporation) for XYZ's review and approval. All schedules in chart form and reports will be reviewed at weekly project meetings and will be included as attachments to each meeting report. Any deviations from these documents will be brought to XYZ's attention by (Design Corporation) for XYZ's review and approval.

All production and construction schedules will be coordinated with any corresponding dates agreed to in XYZ's Lease Documents. Any deviation from these completion dates for whatever cause will be incorporated into the schedules and presented to XYZ for review and approval. When requested, (Design Corporation) will assist XYZ in any negotiations with the Building Owners or Contractors when their concurrence of any schedule is required.

At first glance, many of these provisions may appear unnecessary. For example, of course interior designers will devise a system of cost control and prepare the schedules for the execution of design plans. However, I must emphasize, especially for corporate jobs, how important it is to stress during initial client interviews and in the letter of agreement your vigilance with respect to budget adherance and scheduling compliance.

Recall the comments of the successful architect in Chapter One who advised that corporations are mainly concerned with having their buildings finished at budget and on time. Corporate executives have to answer to stockholders and boards of directors. Frequently, fine quality and innovative design are not as important as relevance and usefulness.

Note that you should volunteer your aid to the client in working with any third parties such as building owners or contractors who are in some way crucial to the operation of the project. It not only makes sense to make these affirmations in writing at the outset of your relationship, it's also the professional way to do business.

Phase Development-Description

The core of most corporate design contracts is the description of the phases on the project. A comprehensive description of a four-phase project will be set forth next. These phases and descriptions represent a pattern of description that is typical of many large corporate design firms. However, keep in mind that these phases can be consolidated or expanded depending upon the scope of the job. The titles of the phases can also be modified or substituted according to the job. The important point is that there is no law or dogma to dictate their titles or descriptions. The titles of the phases and their development need only be clearly written and easily understood. One of the worst mistakes is to prepare a contract with such complex and obtuse language that the client is unable to decipher it. In that case, the designer sometimes loses the job as the client feels he will not know how to work with him.

PHASE I: Programming Analysis
Interior Programming

Working with XYZ's representatives, (Design Corporation) will conduct personal interviews as needed to verify information provided by XYZ. From the information provided by XYZ, (Design Corporation) will develop an interior space utilization program including interpretation of management objectives, space requirements, personal requirements, furnishings, files, special equipment, storage, and departmental adjacency requirements. Summaries of space requirements by departments and sub-department units along with adjacency requirements (Functional Relationships Diagram) will be submitted to XYZ for approval.

Working with these surveys, (Design Corporation) will develop the stacking and block layouts for XYZ's approval.

From the approved program, (Design Corporation) will outline special facilities and/or programs such as food service, acoustics, building security systems, life support systems, etc., that may require special consultants and assist XYZ's representatives in securing these qualified consultants.

Scope Summary:
1. Programming/Space Requirements and Functional Relationships Diagram
2. XYZ Review and Approval
3. Stacking and Blocking Diagrams
4. Client Presentation and Report
5. XYZ Review and Approval
6. Consultant Recommendations
7. Preliminary Budget

For the purposes of this chapter, this corporate design project required the preparation of a functional relationships diagram and stacking and blocking diagrams. These diagrams can be omitted for a simpler project.

There are two important points to note with regard to the Phase I description. First, the client's input and approval are required for all aspects of the development of the interior space utilization program. Always insist on this input and approval, and don't proceed without it. If the client is unhappy toward the end of the project it is important to be able to show him earlier plans that he approved. Second, provide a "scope summary" after the description of each phase. It's obviously much easier to refer to a list so that a potential client can see, step by step, item by item, what he is actually paying for.

PHASE II: Schematics-Design Development
Upon receipt of Phase I approval by the client, (Design Corporation) will undertake Phase II.

Space Planning
Working with XYZ's representatives and with the approved block layouts and stacking plans, (Design Corporation) will investigate various planning concepts and combinations of concepts for the development of space utilization plans.

Working with the approved stacking and block plans, work space requirements, and XYZ's furniture standard, (Design Corporation) will prepare layouts of departments, executive areas, public spaces, etc. showing interior walls, locations of personnel and equipment for XYZ's review and approval. In addition, (Design Corporation) will prepare lighting and power and telephone layout drawings for XYZ's approval.

XYZ will provide for (Designer Corporation) detailed standards of work stations.

Scope Summary:
1. Receipt of Phase I Approval from Client
2. Layout Drawings

3. Lighting and Power and Telephone Drawings

4. Budget Review

5. Presentation

6. XYZ approval

Design Development

Working with the approved concept documents, (Design Corporation) will prepare the following design development drawings to be issued to the architect after XYZ's approval. From these drawings, the building's architect will develop contract documents and specifications for the building's interiors.

1. Architectural Floor Plans

2. Architectural Reflected Ceiling and Light Fixture Switching Plan

3. Power and Telephone Plans
(Design Corporation) will prepare decorative criteria for all interior spaces.

Decorative Criteria, Furniture, and Accessories selections will be submitted to XYZ for approval.

Budgets will be updated to reflect any changes or adjustments in the cost of furniture and equipment. Accessories will be included in the budget.

Scope Summary

1. Design Development Drawings for Building's Architect

2. Decorative Criteria, Furniture, Accessories Schedule and Plans

3. Budget Update

4. Presentation

5. XYZ Approval

Note that prior to the description of the first aspect of Phase II, space planning, it is indicated that Phase II will not commence until the client approves Phase I. There is always some phase overlap in every design project; however, avoid proceeding to the next phase until the prior phase has been approved by your client. Each phase acts as a foundation for the next. If the initial phases are weak, the whole project could collapse.

In the description of space planning, it is stated that the designer will investigate various planning concepts and combinations of concepts for the development of space utilization plans. It is important to use this language in your space planning section to reassure your client that you will consider his ideas, too, until an optimal plan is reached. Although designers usually consider such flexibility an inherent part of the design process, it is important to tell this to a potential client. Corporate clients are usually easier to work for than residential clients because a work space as opposed to a living space is less emotionally charged for the client. However, corporate clients usually make their decisions on a team basis, and your work will usually have to be approved by several executives. It is important to inform the executive in charge of the project in writing that you will consider any and all alternatives that the team members might suggest.

The architect's responsibilities for the project are generally specified in the description of design development. Many interior design projects that involve creating or rebuilding an interior require an architect. In these situations, specify to the client in the letter of agreement what the responsibilities of the architect are. If the architect fails to provide the requisite services later in the project, the designer can at least show his client the contract and request, or even demand, that the architect fulfill his responsibilities.

PHASE III-Contract Documents and Fixture/Furnishings Contract Documents

Upon client approval of Phase II, (Design Corporation) will proceed with Phase III.

Construction Documents

(Design Corporation) will finalize and specify through appropriate and detailed schedules all architectural finishes, including wall coverings, floor coverings, and paint colors, etc., for XYZ's review and approval. Upon approval, XYZ will incorporate these finishes into the construction documents.

(Design Corporation) will prepare carpet plans for issue to the carpet supplier.

(Design Corporation) will provide architectural millwork drawings as required for miscellaneous built-in cabinetry. Minimum cabinetry is expected by XYZ.

(Design Corporation) will review and crosscheck necessary engineering and special consultant's drawings or specifications encompassing structural, electrical, mechanical, and special facilities requirements with the architectural drawings. (Design Corporation) will review the architectural contract documents provided by the building's architect for adherence to the design development drawings prepared by (Design Corporation).

Scope Summary:
1. Receipt of Phase II Approval from Client
2. Finish Schedule Drawings
3. Carpet Plans
4. Architectural Millwork Drawings and Specifications
5. Coordination of Architectural Mechanical and Electrical and Special Consultants' Drawings

Fixture and Furnishings Documents

In addition to the construction drawings described in Phase III, (Design Corporation) will prepare required specifications documents for interior fixtures and furnishings. Based upon approved furniture and furnishings selections developed under Phase II, (Design Corporation) will complete location drawings showing all fixtures and furnishings along with specifications describing all new items in sufficient detail for competitive bidding or negotiation on the particular pieces selected. (Design Corporation) does not purchase and/or handle furniture on a resale basis but will assist in evaluating and reviewing the bids or in negotiations. All purchasing will be in accordance and in conjunction with XYZ's purchasing procedures.

All submittals from furniture manufacturers or dealers will be reviewed by (Design Corporation) for conformance to plans and specifications and copies of reviewed documents with appropriate stamps and notations will be forwarded to XYZ for their records.

Scope Summary:
1. Plans and Specifications for Fixtures/Furnishings
2. Bid Review
3. Bid Item Review and Approvals

Note the careful itemization of the interior designer's duties under *Construction Documents*. This is important for several reasons. First, if you want a client to sign the contract, it's best to enumerate all the things you're going to do for him. Undoubtedly all these items will be mentioned during your initial consultations. But how many of them will your prospective client actually remember? Second, many corporate clients aren't really aware of the vast amount of work involved in a substantial project. The executive in charge of the project may understand how designers operate, but the other executives who must approve his decision probably won't be. Spelling your duties out thoroughly can impress a board of directors when they confer to examine your contract. Third, your contract will state specifically what you will *not* do. As I have mentioned, the interior designer will not purchase any furniture directly. An unsophisticated client might not understand the rationale for this. Therefore, after you have explained it to him, show him how thorough you will be in all other areas. If you can project a seasoned professional image, you can persuade a client to accept one of your operating conditions that he might not like.

There are some very cogent reasons for an interior designer not to purchase furniture for a client or to handle furniture on a resale basis as indicated under *Fixture and Furnishings Documents*. First, the client may not want the designer to make purchases. Many large corporations have their own purchasing agents or use free-lance agents who are paid a commission. If either is the case, find out before the letter of agreement is prepared so you will be able to account for that fact in your contract. Second, some interior designers want to eliminate all the bookkeeping problems that purchasing entails. If a corporate client has its own purchasing department, the designer should prepare the purchase orders and submit them to the purchasing agent or department rather than handle all aspects of purchase transactions including payment, sales taxes, shipping, etc. Third, if the client makes all purchases directly, certain risks of liability are eliminated for the designer. For example, if deliveries are late or the merchandise arrives damaged, the client will look directly to the vendor for replacement or a refund. Naturally, a designer will assist his client in all possible ways, but this method keeps him from being caught in the middle of a quarrel or a lawsuit.

PHASE IV-Construction Coordination

During construction, (Design Corporation) will provide the necessary design coordination and approvals and make periodic visits to the site to familiarize itself generally with the progress and quality of the work and to determine if the work is progressing in compliance with the contract documents and construction schedules.

All site visits will be documented in field reports to keep XYZ apprised of the progress of the construction. (Design Corporation) will review shop drawings for millwork and carpet seaming plans.

Working with XYZ's representatives, (Design Corporation) will assist in the fixture and furnishings installation phase of construction by making periodic site inspections to assure that the installation is in accordance with drawings and specifications.

(Design Corporation) will review and inspect the completed projects after move-in to assist XYZ representatives with any miscellaneous revisions or additions. Revisions and additions are addenda to the base contract.

Scope Summary:
1. Construction Coordination
2. Furnishing Installation Inspection
3. Additional Purchase Items

You have advised us that you will provide (Design Corporation) with plans and specifications that fully describe the buildings in detail.

"Follow-through" and "follow-up" are two of the most frequently used terms in corporate language. When complimented on the design of their offices, corporate executives have been known to comment, "Yes, I suppose the designer designed the space well, but he sure didn't follow up on the project." Your letter must reassure your client that you will do so.

Avoid, however, saying exactly how many site inspections you will make. Different stages of construction will require varying degrees of supervision and, for this reason, visits should be specified as "periodic." To protect yourself against subsequent criticism for inadequate supervision, indicate that visits will be documented in field reports. Send copies to your client. Obviously, inspection visits can become quite tedious in the midst of all the ordinary confusion of construction. However, most experienced designers agree that the extra effort is worth it, especially if after the project is finished, the client complains that he wasn't provided with enough supervision.

The general contractor, not the interior designer, is responsible for the quality and the supervision of the work. Many designers, however, don't want to present a potential client with that in their letter of agreement. They feel that such information will make the client feel that the designer is attempting to avoid responsibility. The letter of agreement in the example infers the absence of designer responsibility for construction by describing the designer's activities to be only those of a *supervisory* nature. If possible, however, I prefer to insert disclaiming language for the quality and supervision of construction in all design contracts.

Fees

Fees were discussed in Chapter Two, and fee structures were compared and analyzed in Chapter One. However, as this chapter traces a commercial contract from start to finish, let us discuss fees at this point, too.

For this particular contract, the design firm chose to keep as far away from its corporate client's internal affairs as possible. In this connection (see Phase III), the design firm refused to purchase any merchandise or, in fact, to assume any responsibility for hiring a general contractor directly. Many corporate designers concur with this philosophy. Even though they may sacrifice large profits by not charging clients on a cost-plus basis, they feel that avoiding liability for purchases and construction enables them to be more objective and finish each job faster. In the long run, these designers believe that they earn more by charging on an hourly basis, using a multiple of direct personnel expense (DPE), as follows:

Professional Fees

We propose to be compensated for services on a timecard basis at a rate of 2.5 times DPE with a not-to-be-exceeded amount of $200,000. All out-of-pocket expenses for reproductions, travel, postage, messengers, long-distance telephone calls and report typing are to be reimbursed at cost. If inflation continues at its present 15 percent to 20 percent annual rate, (Design Corporation) will increase staff salaries to adjust to cost-of-living increases in September 1982. This cost-of-living increase would increase the not-to-be-exceeded amount of $240,000.

Direct personnel expense is defined as the direct salaries of all our technical personnel engaged on the project and the portion of the cost of their mandatory and customary contributions and benefits related thereto, such as employment taxes, and other statutory employee benefits, insurance, sick leave, holiday, vacations, pensions, and similar contributions and benefits.

If after your written approval of documents submitted in Phases I, II, and III, you wish to change them for any reason, any additional services for the change will be performed at a rate of 2.5 times DPE. These are addenda fees that are in addition to the base fee.

As charging DPE is a function of hourly time rates, some clients may be very reticent about salary increases over the life of a project, especially when they are being billed on a multiple. Therefore, note that the design firm used an upset figure of $240,000. Although the project was not intended to be that expensive, the client at least knew that his design fees would not exceed this amount.

Charging by the hour has other advantages. When being paid hourly, designers are compensated for every second they devote to the project. When charging cost-plus, designers have to worry about what is included in their budget for commission purposes. (See Chapter One, *Includable Items.*) Also, under a cost-plus system, clients sometimes make certain designer-specified purchases without his knowledge to avoid paying the design commission. When a designer charges by the hour, it simply doesn't matter what the client buys or when he buys it as far as the designer's compensation is concerned.

Any additions or changes to the documents are billed as "addenda fees." Why use such a term when the hourly rate is the same? The reason is that the upset figure of $240,000 should not be used to strangle the designer financially if the client decides to make endless changes. Therefore, if the $240,000 amount is exceeded because of design additions or changes after the documents have been approved, the designer will no longer be limited to the upset figure.

Photographing Privilege

As indicated in Chapter One, a designer's stock-in-trade is his portfolio and the publicity he receives from being published. Reserve the right, if possible, to photograph completed projects as shown by the following:

> (Design Corporation) reserves the right to exclusively photograph our design work after it is completed and to give permission for its use in any publication although the corporate name will not be used without your consent.

Before you insert this clause in the letter of agreement, sound out the corporate executive in charge of the project.

There are two common corporate objections to the clause. First, some companies don't want their stockholders to see expensively decorated offices. Your promise to withhold the client's identity will usually not be sufficient to allay the fears of corporate executives who are concerned about such exposure. Second, most corporate executives who do want the space photographed will generally not give the designer an "exclusive." For example, executives will want a free rein to photograph all their spaces for brochures and other public relations material. They certainly won't permit themselves to be hamstrung by their designer.

If you encounter any resistance when discussing this aspect of your agreement during initial client interviews, I would omit the clause. If the job is completed to the client's satisfaction, about fifty percent of all clients will permit the designer to let his own photographer photograph the space.

My rationale for urging designers to relinquish this privilege with corporate clients is as follows. Corporate clients are usually much easier to deal with than residential clients. Jobs seem to get finished faster, are less troublesome and more profitable. Also, corporate clients are frequently repeat customers. I have several designer clients who maintain very profitable and secure businesses with only two or three corporate clients. I would not jeopardize losing a valuable commercial client over a photographing privilege.

Arbitration

As indicated in Chapter One, most businessmen, including interior designers, are either sued or have to sue someone at least once during their careers. An arbitration clause in a letter of agreement will usually prevent a lawsuit between designer and client. The advantages of arbitration have already been discussed (See *Avoiding a Legal Crisis*). I want only to remind you that the use of the following clause will result in any disputes between you and your client being settled in an informal, administrative hearing instead of a courtroom:

> Any dispute or disagreement between parties arising out of or relating to this agreement shall be settled by arbitration in (New York) under the rules then obtaining of the American Arbitration Association and judgment upon the award may be entered in any court having jurisdiction.

Although many of my designer clients have either sued or been sued by their residential clients or the vendors and contractors involved, I have never been involved in either a lawsuit or an arbitration proceeding between a designer and a corporate client. This is, of course, not to say that these actions don't occur, but corporate clients really aren't interested in fighting. They're less emotional than residential clients and are basically concerned with having the job completed to specification as scheduled. However, once a corporate client feels that he has been misled by a designer, regardless of the quality of the design and finished product, he will never hire him again.

Closing

The final paragraph is the same one that is used to conclude most letters of agreement (See Chapter One). It can be varied according to your style but should contain the following elements:

If the above meets with your approval, your signature below will indicate your acceptance of the terms of the agreement and will indicate your authorization to proceed with work. Kindly return the duplicate copy to us. Of course, if you have any questions, please don't hesitate to call.

We are looking forward to collaborating with you.

Sincerely,

(Design Corporation)
By: Name of Firm President
President
Dated: September 1, 1981
Agreed & Accepted:

The XYZ Corporation
By: Eugene Smith, Secretary and Director
Real Estate Facilities
Corporate Real Estate Department
Dated: September   , 1981
Agreed & Accepted:

Send the client two signed copies of the agreement. I usually recommend that designers don't begin work until the contract is returned with a signature and some sort of payment. However, with a well-established corporate client, some designers use a different approach. Sometimes they submit preliminary design plans before a contract is prepared. If the client is solid enough, some designers feel that it is a good business risk. This, of course, is a subjective decision to be made on a case-by-case basis.

155

Conclusion

Corporate clients are different from other design clients generally. Nonetheless, the basic rules and concepts for charging and preparing letters of agreement must be absorbed and understood prior to embarking on any variations. Many different ideas and details can be "plugged into" a corporate letter of agreement according to different client needs. I do not bother to outline them in this chapter.

As I have stated earlier, a designer's letter of agreement is a cornerstone of the client relationship. However, as suggested in this chapter, it is important in corporate or commercial situations for a different reason. Residential and other design contracts must be prepared with a somewhat defensive mentality. You want to convince the corporate client of your competence now, not be too preoccupied about protecting yourself from a conflict that might develop later. In any case, before sending out a corporate letter of agreement, make certain that it is concise, well organized, and professional.

CHAPTER FIVE:

Consulting with Clients

This book explains how to run an interior design business from a legal and financial point of view. I have also observed how successful designers consult with clients and acquire new business. Of course, other texts and seminars are devoted entirely to this subject. (See *Mastering and Maintaining Successful Customer Relations for Interior Designers*, Whitney Publications, and *How to Get New Business and Keep Current Clients Sold*, a seminar offered by *Interior Design* Magazine.)

The following material is not intended to be a comprehensive treatment of the subject matter. Nonetheless, I will set forth techniques that can be most effective in aiding designers to consult with clients and will reveal how the experts themselves do it.

Preparing a Portfolio

It is extremely important to own a portfolio that will help you get clients. You must learn what to put in and leave out, what the total effect should be, and how to make yourself look successful and professional. You can study how the experts make their own dramatic statements. Experience will teach what you have to do to capture the client's attention, gain his confidence, and convince him that you are the best possible choice. "Design story emphasis" and "highlighting" can help you to become even more effective.

Although your portfolio evolves continuously, when "finished", its style, look, and flexibility should make a statement that will help successfully close deals.

It isn't a very difficult task for a seasoned interior designer with a number of finished projects under his belt to assemble a portfolio. All completed work should be well photographed, and if the material has been published in shelter magazines, all the better. The real problem arises when a designer is beginning his career and needs a portfolio desperately to attract new clients, as the following example illustrates:

I was consulted by a young interior designer who was just starting his own business with another associate at the same level of experience. After graduating from design school, he had worked for two design firms, a large contract firm and a smaller, creative residential firm. A number of clients had been referred to the designer and his partner, but they lacked a professional portfolio to show prospective clients. They needed to attract new business, not only for the fees but also for the portfolio photographs.

As both designers had worked with firms at which their work had been published, their first step was to assemble all tear-sheets from the magazines of the published articles. In some cases but not all, the designers had been given credit for their participation. They used these articles in their portfolio, explaining to prospects their own participation in each project.

Both designers had kept the projects they had completed in design school, and several of the floor plans looked very professional. The designers had them photographed and reduced in size to fit their portfolio.

After these existing materials were assembled, I met with the designers and gave them a list of techniques that had been used by my other clients for putting together their own first portfolios.

Some designers have their own apartment photographed for their portfolios. It may often be used as a backdrop for a color story. Many designers borrow furniture, accessories, and antiques, from friends or on "memo" or consignment from vendors. They hire a photographer and shoot the rooms from all different angles, styling them in various way using indoor plants and flowers. The same apartment can be made to look like two or three different interiors by a clever designer. A word of caution: Express your own design philosophy but keep it middle of the road. If you have a limited number of photographs and they look too extreme, clients may fear that you lack flexibility. Parenthetically, when showing prospective clients how you live, display an environment to which they can relate, so that they can visualize how some of your elements could be reinterpreted in their own residences.

Photographs of table settings can also be useful additions to a portfolio. They demonstrate the taste and ability of a designer in selecting and assembling accessories. Borrow dining rooms of friends or pursuade vendors to shoot their furniture on showroom floors. Table settings are relatively simple and inexpensive to put together and can be completed within a relatively short period. You can photograph two or three compositions within a matter of weeks.

"Before" and "after" stories fill out a portfolio. A typical favorite is a temporary vacation residence such as a summer beach house. In a rental or newly purchased home, for example, the "before" photograph may show dingy walls and dull furniture. After the space has been painted and inexpensive furniture, accessories, and plants have been added, the "after" photograph will demonstrate your ability. Also, because budgets are generally limited for this type of project, you should say to your client, for example, "I redesigned this rental beach house for $5,000." Resourcefulness on a low budget always creates a positive impression.

Some designers use typical design layouts created from floor plans or photographs of purchased or rented spaces in their area. Then, they create several alternative designs for the same space using black and white and, occasionally, full-color renderings, to illustrate their ideas. If you want to do this but don't draw well, hire a professional. It will be expensive but worth it if the product pleases a client.

Most portfolios contain the designer's resume, a detailed account of his educational and work history. Include a business card, which should have a professional logo using a creative graphic approach. Resume and card are both particularly important if it is necessary to send out the portfolio to a prospective client in a different geographic area.

Once a portfolio becomes substantial, it can be divided into separate volumes—one for residential work and the other for corporate or commercial work. But show all prospective clients both portfolios. A residential client might like an approach used in a commercial project and vice versa. However, separate portfolios illustrate that you have two different areas of expertise.

It is sometimes expeditious to edit a portfolio prior to presentation for a particular client. For example, if you will be meeting with a client who likes a traditional approach, it may be wise to omit some of your contemporary work and substitute photographs of traditional projects that might not otherwise be displayed in your portfolio.

Learning how to assemble a portfolio is an important skill to master, but presenting it properly to potential clients may be of equal importance. A designer should use his portfolio to illustrate his adaptability to the needs of his clients. For example, when showing some of the photographs, point out why certain design decisions were made. For example, contemporary spaces are often designed specifically to accommodate a client's art collection or hobby. Interiors with minimal furniture and neutral backgrounds are often designed for single clients who want environments as maintenance free as possible. Ceramic-tiled kitchen floors and entry foyers are favorites with city apartment dwellers who have limited household help. Rationale such as these should be related when displaying photographs of interiors designed with a specific purpose in mind. Most clients have an infinite permutation of reasons as to why specific design solutions are selected.

Emphasize these reasons when explaining "background" design.

Preparing a portfolio is, to some degree, an acquired skill. But even at the beginning, the more work a designer puts into its development, the better the result will be and the more clients will be attracted.

Consulting with the Client and Getting the Job:

The skill with which you conduct your early client consultations can determine whether you land the account. After a certain amount of practice, you will eventually learn how to develop a relationship over the early phases.

Generally, your contact with a new client will begin with a telephone call. Always ask how you were recommended— a personal or professional contact, a publication, etc. Encourage the client to describe the project: let him do most of the talking. Chances are he will anyway. Be an attentive listener and show enthusiam. Assuming that the phone interview is successful, the next step will be a face-to-face meeting.

This meeting often sets the stage for the entire relationship. The client will size you up. Many designers are uncertain as to how to present themselves at the first meeting as the following example illustrates:

I was consulted by two designers who had formed a partnership after working for small, but well-established design firms for several years. Their former employers were widely published and had impressive offices and large portfolios. The designers told me that their employers generally had one or two brief meetings with prospective clients at which they made little or no sales effort. However, my clients felt that they needed a more assertive approach as they were an unknown quantity as a team. At the same time they wanted to maintain a dignified, professional image. They wanted to know how to "sell" a client in their situation.

Obviously, inexperienced designers may have to use different approaches than their more experienced competitors. For example, you may have to travel to the project site before the client will come to your office for the initial interview. Avoid talking about money until you have personally met with the client, visited the project, and made up your mind as to the best way to charge.

One way to "sell" the client is to outline with a fair amount of precision how you will handle the project. I advised the designers in the example to develop a step-by-step working procedure that would tell a client what he will get for his money. A proper presentation of this procedure can serve two goals. First, it will educate the client about the way a design project operates. (Many don't have any idea about it, having had no prior experience.) Second, it will emphasize that a massive amount of work needs to be done and will clarify the designer's roles and responsibilities.

While most designers have their own specific method of handling a project, here is a typical working procedure that you can adapt as you wish when being interviewed by a prospective client.

Step-By-Step Working Procedure

1. Space Evaluation. Many clients often consult designers before buying or leasing residential and commercial space. At that time, the designer is often encouraged to speak out on various issues, such as "useability of space," esthetic appeal, and the functional aspects of design. Most designers feel much freer to be totally frank about the space *before* the client has taken it. Don't talk a client out of the space if he really wants it. He'll just end up hiring another designer for it. In commercial situations, designers often advise their clients about the conditions for signing a lease—painting, construction, partitioning, flooring, etc.

2. Interview on Space Requirements and Personal Preferences. Clients, especially in residential situations, react to the personal. They love to talk about what they like. They want to be convinced not only of the designer's professionalism but also his responsiveness to what the client wants. There are a number of ways to do this. Many designers ask their clients' "likes," "dislikes," "must haves," and "don't wants." Ask the following questions when you request the preparation of these lists:

a. *Colors.* Do they like pastels or primary hues, bright colors or muted, subdued ones with accents? Do they prefer light living rooms or dark bedrooms? In commercial situations, should colors be incorporated from a company's stationery or packaging?

b. *Style of design.* Do they favor contemporary, traditional, or ultramodern? Some clients have strong preferences; others don't know what they like. Your portfolio should be broad enough so that the client will feel that you can give him what he wants. If it's not, consider showing slides or make up a portfolio with several different styles of rooms.

c. *Materials.* What kind of basic materials does the client like? Does he like marble, wood, or plastic laminate? Does he prefer a traditional approach of taffeta or velvet, or does he prefer the informality of leather and canvas? Some designers elicit these preferences by showing sample boards from previous jobs showing the materials involved.

d. *Lifestyle.* Is the client single, married, or divorced with children? Does he entertain, enjoy cooking, listening to music? What are his hobbies? How does he spend his leisure time? Does he like antiques or collect art? Does he need space for a piano or other musical instrument? Does he own a pet—perhaps a large dog that destroys furniture? Does he have any health problems—allergies or a heightened sensitivity to noise or light? Does he need special accommodations for guests? Does the client insist on a dining table that seats twelve—that will only be used at Thanksgiving? Clients should be thoroughly questioned to determine if their "musts" are really as important as they may initially believe them to be. Would an expandable dining table be more appropriate than a large, permanent dining space that would only be used infrequently.

An extremely important issue for many clients is the amount of storage space. Clients are often obsessed with storage, particularly those who are collectors or compulsive shoppers and savers. You should find out whether the space is for primary or secondary use. It is always important to know how long your client has lived in the space and what he likes or dislikes about it.

e. *Existing furniture or antiques.* What does your

client own now that he wants to put in the newly designed space? Ask for a complete inventory. It is important to know what furniture he has before discussing materials or preparing a visual presentation.

Some clients are better than others about expressing their preferences and making these lists. A designer once told me that her client said in an exasperated tone, "I can't make these lists. I don't know what I like or what I don't like." Ask these particular clients (although you should suggest this to all clients) to submit pictures from books or magazines of interiors that they like. Let them also submit pictures of furniture, window treatments, or rugs, fabrics, etc.

One very important word to the wise. Find out which client is going to be making the design decisions. With married couples, you can usually tell immediately. Single people often have someone in the background whose opinion is solicited before a decision is made. Find out who it is and meet with him from the very first interview. For example, a designer complained that one client made final decisions on Fridays but always changed his mind completely by the following Tuesdays. Finally the client revealed that before signing any purchase orders, he always checked with his business partner to see what he liked.

If you use a project assistant, he should be present at all these initial meetings as well. With corporate clients, you need to know who has final design approval and who issues purchase orders. Request that only one person be designated so that you don't have to answer to several individuals separately.

Most of the above considerations pertain to both residential and commercial situations. Life-style preferences for commercial projects tend frequently to be less exacting because the client is generally more pragmatic. The space must function well and be esthetically pleasing but the client doesn't live there. Of course, at times, especially in partnerships, none of the partners or their wives can agree on what is best for the firm. Apartment building and hotel lobbies are notoriously difficult to decorate for this reason.

3. Survey of Existing Architectural Conditions. Surveying and measuring the space are, of course, prerequisites of any serious design plans. Never rely on building floor plans or existing blueprints. Generally there is no way to vouch for their accuracy, and, if there are errors, you will be held responsible. Tell your client during your early interviews that you will undertake a survey of existing conditions, but make sure your letter of agreement is signed and that you have received a retainer check before you spend time and money. Before even entering your client's premises, obtain appropriate letters from him to the building manager and superintendent (keep a copy for your own files)—these letters are legal safeguards. Naturally, you'll also need a set of keys.

4. Feasibility (Space) Study. As I have emphasized, you have to convince a prospective client that your design ability will satisfy his needs. Your residential client's needs should be researched in the first or second interview as was indicated earlier.

However, in commercial situations, feasibility studies are sometimes quite involved and often don't commence until your client has signed the contract. In the early inter-

167

views, however, you can explain the purpose of a feasibility study and indicate that it takes the following aspects under consideration:

    i. Type of business
    ii. Number of principals involved
    iii. Number of employees
    iv. Number of private offices and departments
    v. Number of clerical and secretarial spaces
    vi. Space requirements for office machinery, computers, telephones and telexes,etc.
    vii. Traffic flow pattern.

Depending upon the type of commercial client, the list can be endless and will vary markedly from business to business. For example, one of my clients, a commercial designer has been frequently retained by brokerage firms to design large specialty desk and telephone systems for traders. During the initial interviews, define the scope of the feasibility study and the nature of its purpose.

5. Visual Presentation. During your first meeting, explain to your client how the visual presentation operates. For example, generally, designers will present a floor plan, furniture layout, some schematic drawings, and even full-color renderings. Material samples and pictures of furnishings may be attached to display boards that mark and describe each area and room. You may display samples of flooring, mirror, wall, and, window treatments, fabrics, pictures of furniture and lighting, etc. The designer should allow sufficient time at the meeting for a complete presentation and should insist that his client earmark the same period of time on his own agenda. All work presented should be thoroughly researched, and the designer should be prepared to answer any questions.

Some designers stage the visual presentation at the design site to enable their clients to easily visualize how the space will look. However, most designers want to conduct the presentation at their own offices. Generally, clients change at least 20 percent of the proposal, and if the designer can show alternatives from examples and catalogues on hand in his office sample room, final decisions are facilitated. It also helps if a member of your staff is available to take notes of client objections and to document the approved changes.

Before the presentation, doublecheck to make sure that all proposed selections are still available. A client of mine once designed a living room and a library and had all selections approved by his client when he discovered to his dismay that most of the selections had been discontinued six months ago.

Some designers provide their clients with a preliminary budget at this stage. If you do, make sure that all prices are current. (The psychology of presenting and discussing budgets has been thoroughly covered under *Charging a Client* and *Dealing with Responsibility.*)

After all substitutions have been resolved, be sure your client indicates his final approval by initialling all sample boards and other presentation memoranda.

6. Preparation of Construction and Cabinet Drawings. Most prospective clients are unfamiliar with the amount of work that goes into a full set of working drawings. Accordingly, many designers show them a sample set from another project, so that they can understand what is entailed. For commercial projects, unless the designer is being hired only to decorate some of the spaces, the following list is typical of the drawings included in a sample set:

i. Existing conditions
ii. Demolition
iii. Construction
iv. Reflected ceilings
v. Electrical and telephone
vi. Finish schedules (paint and wallcoverings)
vii. Cabinet work
viii. Hardware

Advise your clients that this is probably the costliest and most difficult phase of the project, as drafting is expensive and time-consuming.

Don't prepare extensive, detailed cabinet drawings for residential projects unless you are fairly certain that the client wants to finance the construction to implement the plans. In their enthusiasm about a total design concept, some designers prepare all the drawings without first obtaining preliminary estimates. When the contractors bid on the job and the client balks at the cost, all the work has been wasted.

If clients are shown sample sets of drawings during initial consultations, they often complain that they cannot interpret them. Explain that you will take them to the project and measure out furniture and cabinet work with tape or chalk so they can visualize your designs. Remind them also that you will supply a rendering and sketches at the visual presentation.

Once the drawings have been reviewed and approved by the client, send them out to the contractors for written bids. A dated cover letter should accompany them and include any last-minute changes not incorporated, perhaps, on the drawings. Before sending the drawings out, notify the contractors selected in advance, so that they will be aware that your drawings are being submitted for bid. Specify a deadline date. Tell your client that you can't proceed on the project until all bids are received, so that he won't make any needless revisions or additions until the budget figures have been analyzed.

The next three steps—seven through nine—do not usually have to be explained in great detail in the initial client consultations. Brief summaries for each step are now provided for purposes of continuity and information—if, in fact, a prospective client does question you about them in greater depth.

7. Review and Evaluation of Construction and Cabinet Bids. Once all bids have been received from contractors and subcontractors, most changes and eliminations will, usually, be made for budget reasons. Clients often eliminate some of their earlier "needs and requirements" once they see hard budget figures. Bids are analyzed, changes are finalized, and contractors and subcontractors are consulted again to determine the revised budget.

8. Submission of Final Budget. After the final construction, cabinet work, and furnishings budgets have been revised, they should be carefully organized and presented to the client at a final meeting. Don't forget to include sales tax and delivery charges. Further, some designers add an additional ten percent contingency in the event of price increases or substitutions.

9. Preparation and Issuance of Purchase Orders on All Goods and Construction. Systematically incorporate everything from the budget(s) on all purchase orders; be careful not to leave anything out. Usually the most complex purchase order or series of purchase orders will be the one(s) for construction. Some designers use their floor plans and prepare the orders on a room-by-room basis.

If you intend to act as the client's agent for payment, you will usually prepare an estimate for him, and he will forward you a deposit as required. Then, you will prepare a purchase order to be sent directly to the vendor.

If the client is going to make his own purchases and payments, you will prepare the purchase orders for his use in triplicate. One copy is retained for your files; another is forwarded to the vendor by the client, and a third is kept by the client for his own files. Have the client initial your copy indicating his approval. This is extremely important for the reasons cited in detail in Chapter Three.

When forwarding these purchase orders to the client, many designers wisely include a covering letter as the following example illustrates:

Date

Dear (Name of Client):

Attached please find enclosed purchase order

#_____, dated: January 15, 1981. Please send

one copy of your check directly to the vendor and fill in
the following information for our records:

> Amount of Check:
> Name of Vendor:
> Name of Bank and Check Number:
> Please process this letter as soon as possible
> to enable our office to check on your order.

> > Very truly yours,

> > > Name of PRINCIPAL of Design Firm

Once the covering letter has been returned to you, you
will know that the order has been processed and will be
able to check up on it if necessary.

Before preparing any orders, ask your client what name
should be listed as the "purchaser." For example, some
residential clients may instruct you to list their business
as the "purchaser" for tax reasons. Accordingly, don't prepare the orders before checking with the client to avoid the
possibility of having to redo them because the incorrect
name was used.

**10. Job Supervision and Implementation of De-
sign.** Although your letter of agreement will state that the
responsibility for the quality and supervision of the construction is the obligation of the general contractor, advise
prospective clients that you will be at the job site as necessary with an original set of working drawings to make any
on-the-spot changes if unexpected field conditions arise.
For example, if recessed cabinets are to be installed after
demolition of a wall, a beam might unexpectedly become
revealed that would prohibit that sort of installation. You

must, as the designer, make the necessary adaptation.

11. Move-in Supervision. A discussion of "move-in" at initial meetings can have a very positive effect. With a large, vague project looming before him, a client likes to feel that project completion is a forseeable reality. Advise your client that deliveries of furniture can be handled in two ways. It is best to warehouse all the goods at one centrally located warehouse until you are ready to make one final installation. Clients are often disquieted by piecemeal deliveries. Each piece may look "wrong" until all the furnishings are put together. If your client will not allow you to do this, try at least to arrange for all major deliveries to be made within a one-week period.

Your step-by-step procedure is one of the most valuable selling tools for impressing a prospective client. If retained, of course, you will request a retainer and set forth your client's financial commitments in a contract. It only makes sense to sell the client on the amount of work, time, and professional skill that is necessary to undertake and complete the job.

How to Look Professional—What the Experts Do

The art of interviewing and being interviewed is refined by years of experience. Although most designers have the same objective during initial meetings—to inspire confidence, trust and communication—they all have their own styles and techniques of presentation.

The following interviews, taken from a cross-section of residential and contract designers selected by *Interior Design*, present various points of view about handling prospective clients during initial meetings.

174

Braswell-Willoughby, Inc. Joseph Braswell, ASID, whose eclectic designs suit the varying tastes among his clients, shows his portfolio selectively. He wouldn't, for example, show the elaborate design created for a Saudi Arabian palace to a couple who own a simple country house.

At the first meeting, he tries to ascertain whether his firm and the client are right for each other. "You're foolish to think," he adds, "that you can do everything. Take an inventory of your own potential. It's hard for a person to know his limitations, but you have to try."

One of his most important objectives is to create an impression of flexibility. In doing so, he finds that the subtle nuances of a client's taste will be revealed. For example, if a client mentions that he doesn't want a "formal living room," Mr. Braswell will probe gently to find out the client's definition of that term. Often, he advises, it will have no relation to the "design definition." What's important is to let the client know that he is understood. That, Mr. Braswell feels, will earn his confidence.

He is friendly with prospective clients but maintains some social distance to preserve objectivity and a clinical attitude. If a client subsequently turns out to be a neurotic who makes ten hysterical telephone calls to his office each day, he will tell him, after all other efforts fail, "Please try to relax. It's only decorating."

Ellen L. McCluskey Associates, Inc. Budget is a threshold issue with Ellen McCluskey, FASID. An immediate evaluation will be made with regard to the general budget and the value of the space. If the cost will be too high for the result—for example, for a space to be used on a temporary basis—the client will be candidly advised that the expense "simply isn't worth it."

The amount of work devoted to preparation for initial interviews depends upon the client. If the potential project is a large one, plans may be quite elaborate. Slide presentations may be assembled and edited, based upon the needs and wants of the client as disclosed during early conversation. Other factors influence the amount of input devoted to plans for interviews. For example, if a prospective client must have bank approval for financing before the project can commence, preliminary design plans may need to be prepared before a contract is signed. Of course, the client must pay for this work.

On occasion, a detailed proposal may be prepared on speculation for a large contract job. In one case, a full-color rendering was prepared at considerable expense, and the firm won the job.

The McCluskey office emphasizes the contrast between the contract and residential projects. "Residential clients are more esthetically oriented. A personal relationship is important, a firm principal must be involved, and the client is more 'result oriented.' Contract clients, on the other hand, want to be sure that the firm understands how their business operates. They are more interested in the mechanics of the design process than the residential client and like to be assured of a complete 'staff back-up' so there will be no standstill on the job. These concepts are carefully instilled during early conversations to enable a prospective client to understand that the firm is capable of responding to its requirements."

Bebe Winkler Interior Design. Bebe Winkler, ASID, advises that "in about 80 percent of my client interviews, the client is generally pre-sold on my design ability. They usually come to me as a direct referral." For example she has four residential clients who live not only in the same suburb but on the same street. "Their interiors will all be totally different. Each client wanted to hire me because he saw that what I was doing for the others was so completely personal. They felt confident that I would be able to understand them as well."

Ms. Winkler has definite ideas about interviews. She generally insists on an office visit before she will visit the site. If the client is a married couple, she prefers that both husband and wife attend the first meeting. This will enable her to demonstrate to the husband that she is a competent business woman as well as a talented designer.

Ms. Winkler prefers that the initial interview take place at her office. "I feel much stronger in my own domain. But I never sit at my desk; I usually sit somewhere on the sidelines to create a more informal atmosphere." Once in a while she'll make an exception about the office interview if a prospective client tells her on the phone, "I have a lot of things that I want you to consider working with." This statement, she feels, might be a danger signal that should bear some investigation before any serious interviewing is done. In any event, she curtails interviews after an hour and a half because they become "counterproductive" at that point.

Unlike some designers, she doesn't show prospective clients her finished work. "If they know my other clients and have seen their projects, fine. But if they don't know them, they may have no idea why I used that approach at all." This philosophy is the hallmark of a designer who convinces prospective clients from the outset that the design will be tailored for them, not merely a variation of her previous work.

Maurice Weir Designs, Inc. Walter Waller, ASID, has lined the walls of his office with many framed color renderings of projects completed over the years. As a result, his office has the distinct ambience of an art gallery. He prefers not to show clients photographs from a portfolio, which, he feels, "looks a little like you're just out of school." If a client wants to see photographs, he has many large-scale ones mounted on boards. These can be picked up, held up to light, revealing design elements with an extraordinary sense of reality.

During the initial interviews, he will present himself as flexible. "Clients are reassured if you let them know that you're looking for a solution that pleases *them.* After all, it's their apartment, not ours. Of course, we do want to design it in the best possible taste."

Mr. Waller feels that the detective work of discovering prospective clients' preferences is an intriguing aspect of interviewing. Clients are told that the firm cannot undertake the project with an "impossible budget." Complete candor, he believes, prevents unrealistic financial commitments. "Why start something you can't finish?" he emphasizes. "We can't complete a twenty-by-thirty foot living room for $10,000." He does tell new clients, however, that their money will be watched carefully and that all aspects of the project will have a complete follow-through. "It is important to tell clients that there are at least 100,000 design elements and that we keep track of them all."

Dexter Design, Inc. Barbara Ross asks potential clients whether they want a totally redesigned and updated space. "Clients rarely admit how much they've got to spend, so I tell them that a new, wonderful room with new windows will cost a minimum of $50,000." This honesty shocks many clients who haven't had a space designed in five years or more. However, this honesty endures through the entire relationship, and she warns new clients, "This is no glamorous love affair . . . it's a bumpy road."

She and her partner, Barbara Schwartz, ASID, try to recognize the type of individual who will want to make a full-time career of his project. They tell new

179

clients that a time limit will be placed on the project because, "after all, a designer's enthusiasm can't last over a period of years." Nonetheless, they find that most of their clients eventually become personal friends.

Unlike many other designers, they don't believe that "researching" prospective clients in advance is the answer. "We'd rather use our intuition based upon their immediate responses and prefer to rely on the chemical reaction of the first meeting. The energy of spontaneity is obvious."

And unlike other design partners, they don't always present a united front. Barbara Schwartz freely admits, "Barbara and I come on like gangbusters, and new clients either like us or they don't. We often disagree about decisions in front of prospective clients to show them how the process works."

They are very direct about the scheduling of jobs as well. If, for example, a new client is in a hurry, they'll be careful to tell him before the contract is signed if they're overloaded with work and can't begin before a specific date. If a client is vague about proceeding with a job, he will be asked if he plans to retain them or not. If he wants time to think things over, he'll be asked for a decision date.

Interviewing prospective clients is a very exciting part of their business. Barbara Ross believes, "There's a certain amount of 'show biz' in every project. It's almost a part of theatre, and we like to perform. After all, we are doing something major for our client's life."

Jack Lowery and Associates, Inc. Jack Lowery, FA-SID, the national president of the ASID, presents his portfolio creatively to prospective clients. He included photographs of a "way-out" bank in a recent slide presentation for a retail store because, Mr. Lowery comments, "a bank *is* a store, after all." He feels that if a young designer has had no experience with a particular type of project, e.g., a hospital, he shouldn't try to fake it. The best thing to do is to show your joy and anticipation about the project and let the client do most of the talking, especially when you don't have a lot to say." Of course, he encourages emphasizing other completed projects with similar operational aspects. "Even experienced designers," he notes, "haven't done everything . . . why, we're not supposed to . . . but we are supposed to do some fast homework to find out how to do it." When confronted with a new challenge, he recommends calling friends and colleagues with more experience and even joint venturing with them if necessary.

If he decides to take a client to the actual site of a completed project, an infrequent practice, he will always visit the site by himself first to make sure it looks the same way it did when he finished it. "Sometimes former clients will have allowed their space to deteriorate or will have even changed it, but a visit with a prospective client is not the time to find that out."

Prior to interviewing corporate clients, he likes to investigate their background and "know my cast of characters." Middle management may solicit the initial interview; however, "senior people sit in on these meetings, and it's important to be prepared for them."

During the initial interview, he will decide what he and his staff have to offer the potential client. A small firm can emphasize personal service when competing against the big ones. Accordingly, he will couch his comments and presentation to lead up to the "big moment."

Significantly, Mr. Lowery mentions that when the client feels comfortable with the designer, the deal is almost clinched. "It means being interested and being an interesting person on a conversational level with a client that you like. It's the joint experience of solving a problem."

Forbes-Ergas Design Associates, Inc. Susan A. Forbes, ASID, and Joel M. Ergas, ASID, agree that during the initial interview, it is important to learn how clients "put themselves together." However, because many clients do not express all their desires, "we have to show them something that they can respond to." For example, during an interview, the designers may do quick sketches, working drawings according to a client's description. "This shows our involvement. . . . We're not worried about having our brains picked and giving something away for free, we want to show that we're concerned principals."

They also know how to reassure an uneasy client.

"Color and materials are very important to people, but many corporate clients don't think about such matters. They think about the space, whether it is brand new, an expansion, etc. So we show some clients color and material boards right away. If the client is strictly 'literal,' we will show him only what he talks about. We may show other clients many things to stimulate their imagination. This judgment must be made on the spot."

Large corporate projects, they point out, are sometimes never built even though the designer may be paid for the complete design plans. "For some projects, there may be weeks of screening. Finally we have to decide—once we are retained—if we feel that project will be built or shelved. It can be a tough decision when you have a fabulous project but no client. Even so, all completed and photographed design plans can still be very useful for our portfolio."

Occasionally, they will undertake a challenging project even if the design fee and budget are low because the result will be helpful for their portfolio. They cite as an example the design of a small, exciting restaurant. "For a new designer that approach can 'make his name in that area.'"

For corporate work, they try to determine during the first few interviews whether, "we can pull the client together and develop a cohesive point of view." They remember a hotel for which the director wanted extravagant glamour but the financial management imposed budget restrictions. "If there are too many divergent management positions, it may be just too much to organize all that energy and put it into one voice."

They emphasize the need to talk to a corporate client in specific terms. It is important, they add, for new designers to become totally familiar with the language of materials, architecture, lighting, and to make this clear to the client from the beginning. "Clarity is so important. We don't try to sell a mystique or superficially describe the end product as 'having a nice look.' We do not want a surprised client."

Walker/Group, Inc. Kenneth H. Walker, AIA, shows potential clients reprints from the trade and general press of his completed projects. "I capitalize on past work. The media has been very kind to my firm, which has been provided with a broad variety of useful ammunition." He also has a massive slide collection at his disposal and employs one person solely to maintain a slide library. Much effort goes into a slide presentation for a prospective client that shows more than completed projects. "We use slides to address ourselves to the client's problem so that he'll know we understand." These slides might include cityscapes, a marketplace in Peru, automobile interiors, lighting examples, or funny slides that make people laugh. ("We use a picture of a slave ship to illustrate overcrowding in an office, and even famous pictures like 'The Last Supper.'")

Mr. Walker emphasizes the importance of clients coming to his office to meet his staff. "There is a big stake in introducing personnel to prospective

184

clients. We like to advertise the stability of our staff; there is a suprisingly low turnover."

He believes that small firms can use their size as an advantage. "Although we're large now, we used to be small not that long ago. In a small firm, the principal can meet with prospective clients and sell the hell out of its projects. Now, I just can't be every-where. Big firms are stretched."

"Another big issue," he advises,"is whether the firm is going to be one 'individual' or 'several indi-viduals.' I always meet potential clients with my staff, never by myself. We show 'people, continuity, experience.' That convinces clients as to our hones-ty."

Mr. Walker believes a design firm should carefully assess what it has to sell to a potential client. "In our case, design is the main issue. But that is not true for 80 percent of the design firms that do cor-porate work. If you're a great facilities planner, sell that. Or if you're great at working with tight time schedules, sell that. Analyze what you have and cap-italize on it."

When asked if he used a special technique in order to be retained by a particularly attractive client, his reply was "a sense of humor. There's always a lot of money at stake, and we're going to be living with our clients for a long time. When we can make a client laugh, we're ahead of the game."

Patricia Harvey Interiors. Patricia Harvey, FASID, watches carefully during the first interviews to see whether a potential residential client wants a "slick magazine look" or is primarily interested in comfort. "Women, as well as men, are more interested in comfort today than ever before. So many women work full time and want to be able to relax at the end of the day. Even many younger people revolt at the thought of a multi-level platformed living room. If I sense that, I will emphasize at the end of the meeting that their house will look like a 'home' with certain areas designed for comfort."

When consulting with a married couple, she also points out that age can be an important factor. Often older couples will contact her when they are disposing of a large family house or apartment, moving to a smaller residence, or acquiring a second residence, perhaps in a warmer climate. "Either the husband or the wife thinks the move will be traumatic. At that point, I offer reassurance to show that I understand what they're going through, that they're doing the right thing. I often respond, 'Oh, how nice. You're going to unclutter your life.'"

She also always analyzes whether a potential client will enjoy working with her on a personal level before undertaking the project. "Some women don't want to work with other women," she points out. "When Arthur Murray, the famous dance instructor, came to consult me without his wife Katherine, I knew it wouldn't work. She's a 'man's woman,' and I referred him to a male designer who was a friend of mine."

On one occasion, she remembers a potential male client who didn't want to work with a woman. A

well-known Saudi Arabian sent his male secretary
to her office. "He wanted to see Pat Harvey. And
when I said, 'I'm Pat Harvey,' he said, 'Oh, I see,'
bowed politely, and left. I saw a $400,000 job going
out the door."

John Gerald Associates, Inc. "I'm a retail salesman
with a lot of imagination," John Gerald tells potential clients. Mr. Gerald, a elder statesman of interior
design, a former Executive Vice-President of W&J
Sloane and one-time owner of Hammacher Schlem-
mer, is the master of understatement. He has been
in business for over fifty years; his corporate and
residential clients include the rich and famous who
don't want publicity. "But we don't need it, we're
awfully spoiled . . . we take what we want."
     When interviewing a prospective client, he ad-
vises, "Tell them the truth, and keep it low key. I
never use an 'up-and-at-'em' approach. People have
heard all about 'decorators,' so they're frightened to
begin with. I often tell a couple that the wife could
probably do a good job, too."
     John Gerald leads his clients slowly; he thinks
carefully before making suggestions at the first or
second meeting. "Never start by telling them to
throw everything out," he cautions, "it's like raising
a red flag with a bull. You have to know how far to
go with a client." He believes that clients don't like
being pushed, that they resent it throughout the relationship, and that the wrong type of aggressive-
ness can build up animosity between the client and

the designer. "Maybe a rich old aunt gave (the client) an ugly desk and they have to keep it. They might not admit it at first, but they'll tell you later on."

Part of his approach is to "talk common sense in plain language. Most men don't know the difference between raised panels and applied moldings. When they look at furniture, which is *always* too expensive, I always ask what kind of car they drive."

When it comes to money, he forces his clients to "come clean. I ask them how much they'll spend and not to hold back. If they say, 'Well, $50,000, maybe a little more,' I'll say, 'How much more?'" Mr. Gerald says money isn't too much of a problem with his clients. "I will not make a presentation without the husband. And, I'll always give him comfort. Recliners appeal to a man."

Being gentle with a potential client doesn't mean being subdued. "It's always fine to be encouraging," he adds. "Be enthusiastic and tell them how *wonderful* and how *beautiful* things will look when they're finished."

When asked why most of his business is repeat, he replies, "because my interiors are timeless. The trouble is that 'good' goods really are 'good' goods. They last forever. But quality will save you in the end. And, above all, you need good taste. I make sure my clients use only *white* candles on the dinner table."

Neville Lewis Associates, Incorporated. Neville Lewis, ASID, suggests that it isn't easy to isolate the specific ingredient that will earn client confidence at the first few interviews. The founder of the contract design firm, an office that, although only a few years old, employs fifty men in New York, twenty in Denver, and twenty in Dallas, recalls, "the biggest problem we had when we started was that we had nothing to show. That was a disadvantage. But when we were interviewed by an insurance company, we prepared preliminary design plans on speculation and got the job. Now, we only do that rarely; I don't like to get trapped into it." But the presentation alone, he feels, is not what captures a prospective client. "It's the chemistry . . . if they like you, pictures don't mean a thing. Sometimes, they don't want to be convinced, and it's all a waste of time. I don't want to sell anything we're not."

Although Mr. Lewis has no prescription for clinching deals, he follows certain policies during the first few interviews. First, a presentation, he feels, should be thorough and professional but not overdone. "We don't believe in a 'flash' presentation, it's too phony . . . anyone can do it." Second, he advocates using a straightforward approach. "Clients are sophisticated now, and we don't talk down to them. They know all the answers. We're up against top people, and all the presentations are good, so we try to convince new clients that we'll come in on schedule and under budget. We are all talking together at the end of a job." Third, he thinks his clients want to see a united front from a design office. His personnel do not express divergent opinions at initial meetings. Fourth, he warns against creating a "designer signature look," an ego trip that corporate clients abhor, and advises reassuring a client that the result will be appropriate for them. "U.S. Steel," he comments, "is not supposed to look like Revlon." Fifth, he urges designers to be responsive. "Find out who is going to be at the meeting. Be honest but put things in the right way. Don't embarrass a corporate employee in front of his superiors if he has provided some inaccurate information. This, Mr. Lewis reflects, is all part of being prepared. "If you get fat and happy and do a canned presentation, clients will read right through it." Sixth, "Let the client know you're going to be there—and I don't always know how you can always get that across . . . but it's a response business. They don't teach you that in school. Do something for your client."

And finally, Neville Lewis says, "Get a reputation as being a clean outfit. If you keep that, you'll get your share of the work. It's probably worth more than anything else you've got to offer."

These interviews clearly illustrate that these experts disagree sharply on techniques. They all have their own styles that suit their clientele and mesh with their own personalities. But, their objectives are similar, and they all are complete professionals.

Conclusion

As I have stated many times, the information presented here, although fairly comprehensive, is not exhaustive on each topic. That would be impossible. I have raised those issues that most frequently confront the designers whom I have counseled during my career as a legal and business adviser.

An interior design business must be flexible. Different circumstances can often mandate different approaches. I have not set out formulas for you to follow or programs for you to adhere to by merely substituting or "plugging in" your own facts. Instead, I have tried to show you various approaches to problems, why these approaches might be implemented, and how they can be varied. Memorizing the actual situatons has little value. Understanding the decision-making process is the whole key.

Developing the skill to manage your business properly is not merely a convenience or energy-saving advantage. It is worth money. Money can mean the difference between prospering or surviving, between success or failure. If you earnestly attempt to analyze and apply the principles set forth here to your own business, there will be no doubt about it. You will make more money.